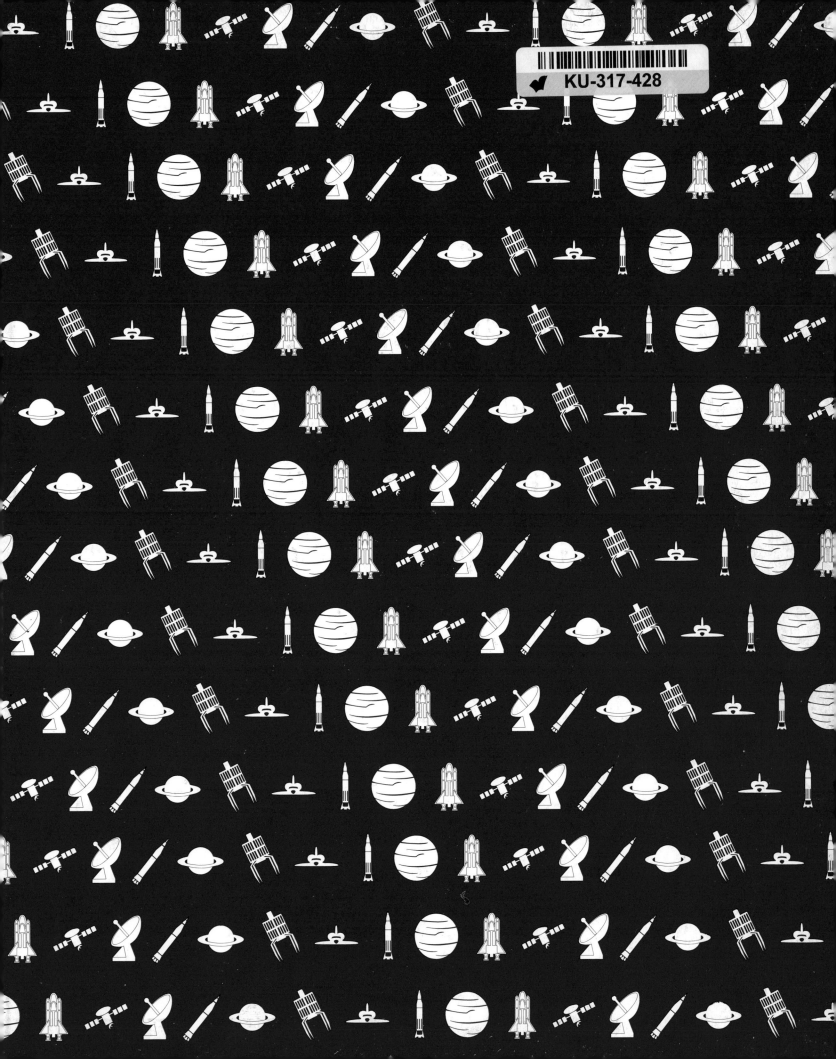

# EXPLORING SPACE

DAVID SHAYLER

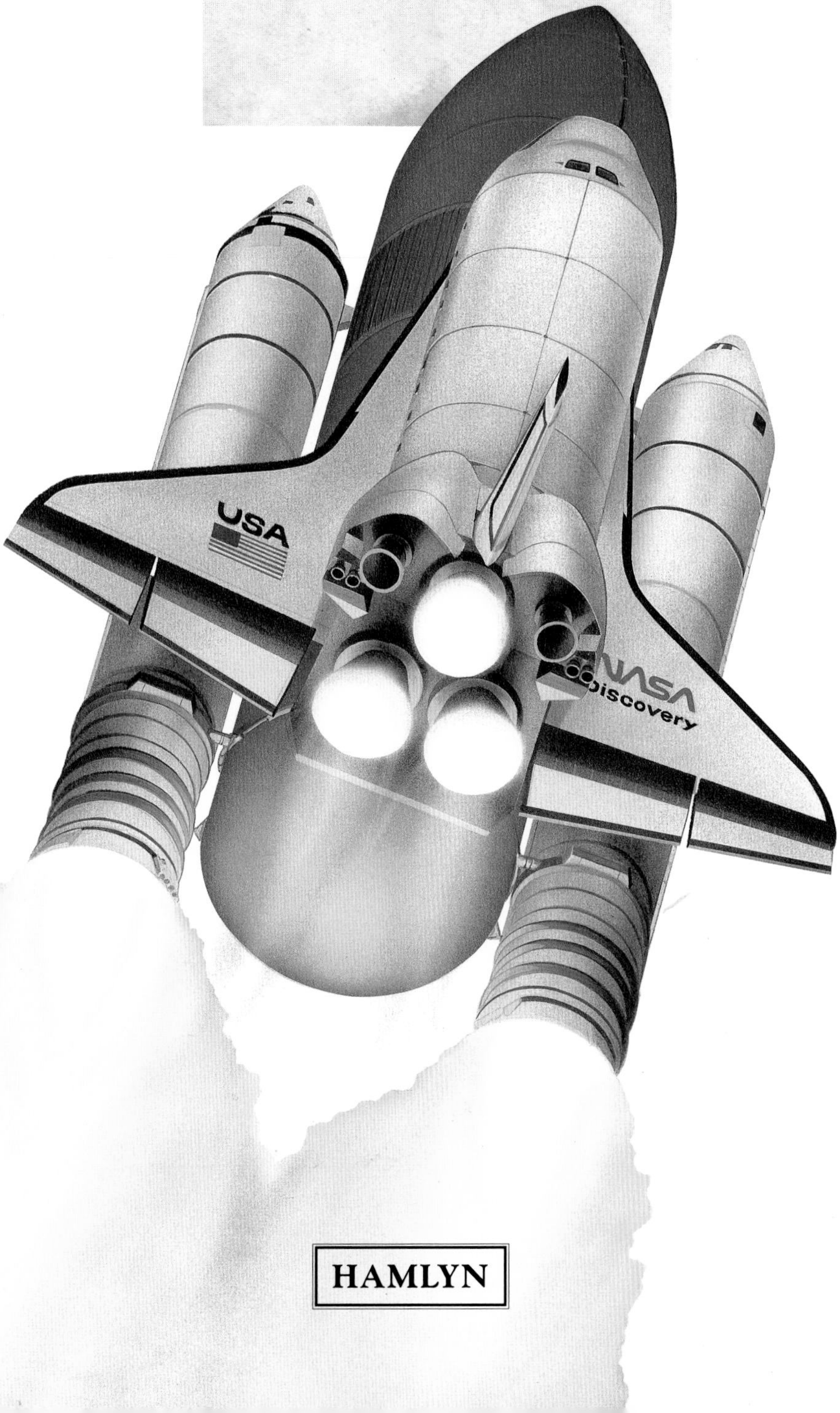
USA
NASA
Discovery

HAMLYN

## FOREWORD

'Reading through the pages of this book caused me to think about the great fun of making a spaceflight. I well remember the bone-rattling lift-off, the rocket's push accelerating us beyond the edge of the Earth, the sudden silence of these same engines as they shut down and then the eerie quiet of coasting in unending orbit around our beautiful planet.
I hope you enjoy reading this book as much as I have.'

Joe (Joseph) Allen
Mission specialist on Space Shuttle missions STS-5 and 51-A.


## ACKNOWLEDGEMENTS

The author and publisher would like to thank Joe Allen, President of Space Industries International; Dave Portree and many others at the various NASA facilities; Neville Kidger; Andy Salmon and Mike Shayler, for their assistance in the preparation of *Exploring Space*; and the following individuals and organizations for their kind permission to reproduce the photographs used in this book:
Boeing: 32 bottom left. Britstock-IFA Ltd: 11 top. Genesis Space Photo Library: 27 top (NASA), 31 top right. Michael Holford: 4. Neville Kidger: 40 centre. Kobal Collection: 6 left. NASA: 9 bottom, 10, 14, 21 bottom, 21 top, 24 left, 26, 27 bottom, 28 top, 29 left, 29 top right, 32 top, 32 centre right, 34 bottom left, 39. Quadrant Picture Library: 13 right, 24 right (NASA). Scala (Museo della Scienza, Firenze): 5 bottom left. Science Photo Library: 5 top (Roger Ressmeyer, Starlight), 5 bottom right (Chris Butler), 7 bottom left (NASA), 8 left (NASA), 9 top (Novosti), 15 bottom (R. Ressmeyer, Starlight), 16 bottom (NASA), 22 centre (R. Ressmeyer, Starlight), 28 centre (NASA), 28 bottom (R. Ressmeyer, Starlight), 29 centre (NASA), 30-31 (NASA), 34 bottom right (Tony Ward, Tetbury), 40 bottom left (R. Ressmeyer, Starlight), 44 (R. Ressmeyer, Starlight), 45 (David Hardy). Space Commerce Corporation: 40 top right. Starland Picture Library: 11 bottom left (NASA), 13 left (ESA), 29 bottom right (NASA). TASS: 20. Telegraph Colour Library: 18, 37. Topham Picture Source: 6 right, 15 top (AP), 38.

## ILLUSTRATORS

Arcana: 8, 9, 15, 20, 44 bottom right, 46-47. Julian Baker: 6-7, 7, 10, 11, 12 bottom, 16, 17, 24, 25, 33, 41. Peter Bull: 12 top, 14. Joe Lawrence: 30, 34-35, 36, 37, 38-39, 44 top right, 45 top left. Maltings Partnership: 4-5, 8-9, 20-21, 22-23, 26-27, 42-43, 45 bottom. Brian MacIntyre: 18-19. Ed Stuart: 6 bottom left and right, 31, 35, 39 bottom, 42.

First published in Great Britain 1994
by Hamlyn Children's Books,
an imprint of Reed Children's Books Limited,
Michelin House, 81 Fulham Road, London SW3 6RB,
and Auckland, Melbourne, Singapore and Toronto.





ISBN 0 600 58199 3

A CIP catalogue record for this book is available at the British Library.

# CONTENTS

# WATCHING THE SKIES

**Humans have watched the skies from the earliest times. The most visible objects were the Sun and Moon. They were worshipped as gods and goddesses, and became part of myths and legends.**

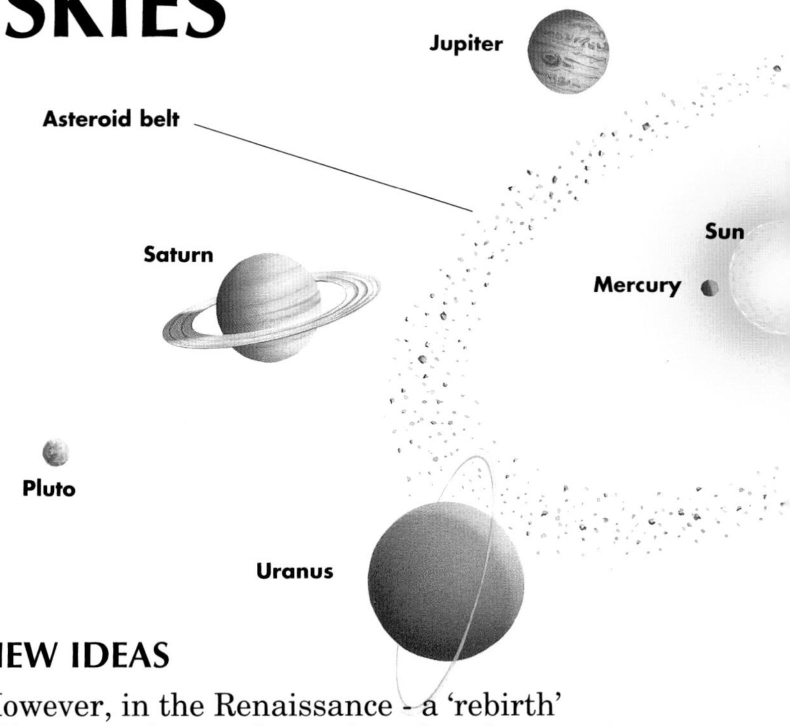

Jupiter
Asteroid belt
Sun
Saturn
Mercury
Pluto
Uranus


## ASTROLOGY

The stars and planets, too, were part of the mysterious world beyond the reach of humans. The movements of these 'heavenly bodies' seemed to herald important events, such as the start of spring, or a time of floods. Many people believed the stars and planets controlled all events on Earth. Some of them, called astrologers, tried to predict the future by studying the skies.

In ancient Greece, the astronomer Aristarchus worked out that these stars and planets did not travel around the Earth, but that the Earth moved in the sky. Most people did not believe him. For over a thousand years most people believed the Earth was the centre of the Universe. Everything else - the 'heavenly bodies' - was placed there by God to service the needs of the Earth and Man.

## NEW IDEAS

However, in the Renaissance - a 'rebirth' of learning during the 14th and 15th centuries - scholars rediscovered the ideas of the ancient scholars. Astronomers such as Copernicus in Poland, Kepler in Germany, Galileo in Italy and Newton in England worked out the movements of the Earth and other planets. They found that all of them revolved around the Sun. This work laid the foundations for the logical, scientific study of the Universe.

ISTI MIRANT STELLA
HAROLD


*The passing of a comet, probably Halley's Comet, is recorded in the Bayeux Tapestry (right). This Norman tapestry was woven in France in the 11th century. Over 2,000 years ago, the ancient Chinese and Egyptians charted the movements of the stars out to Jupiter and Saturn. The outer planets of our solar system were discovered many years later: Uranus in 1781, Neptune in 1846 and finally Pluto in 1930.*

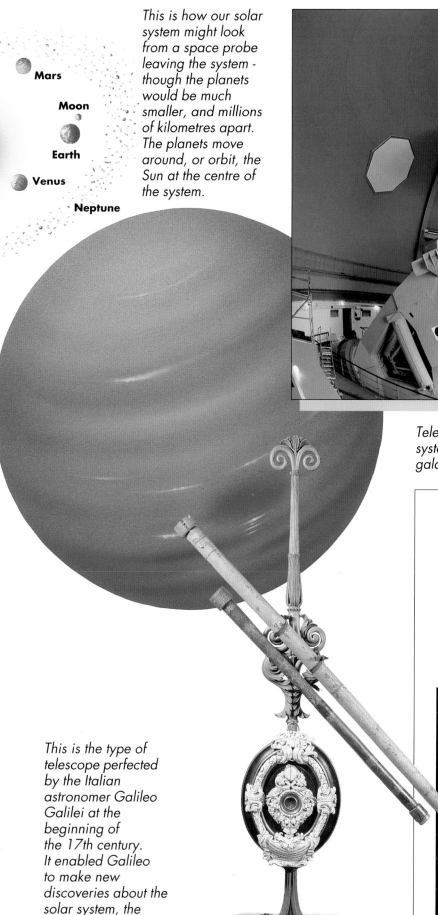

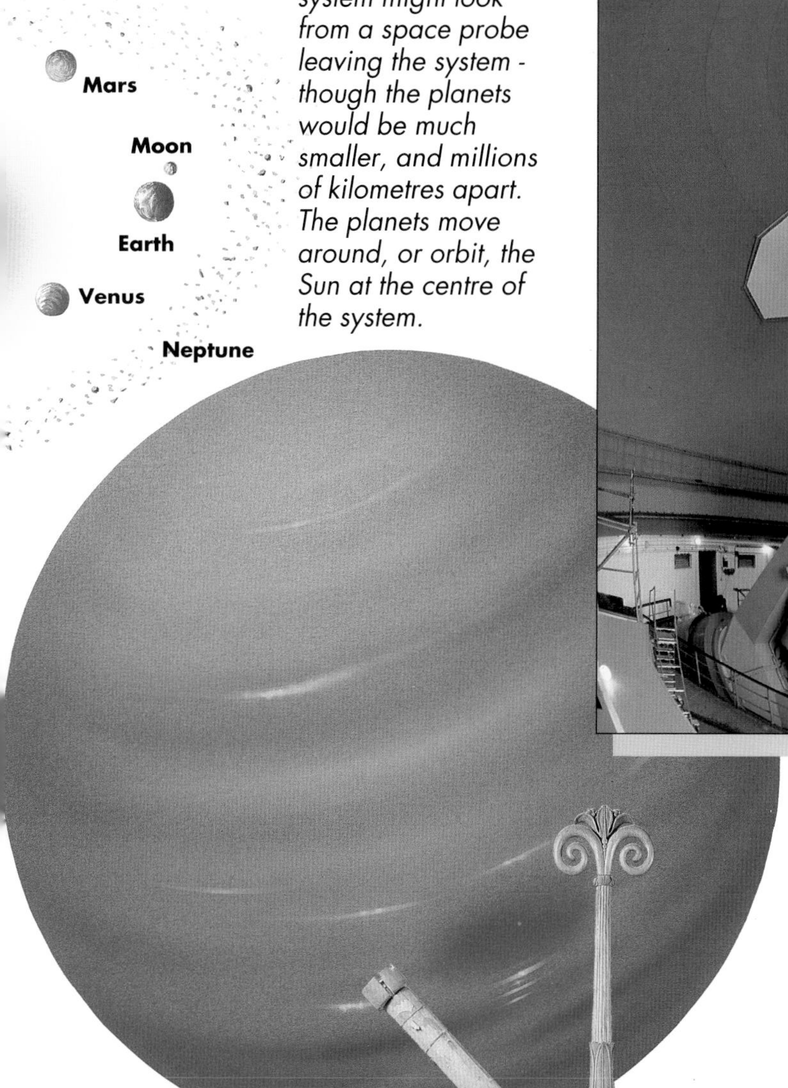
Mars
Moon
Earth
Venus
Neptune

*This is how our solar system might look from a space probe leaving the system - though the planets would be much smaller, and millions of kilometres apart. The planets move around, or orbit, the Sun at the centre of the system.*

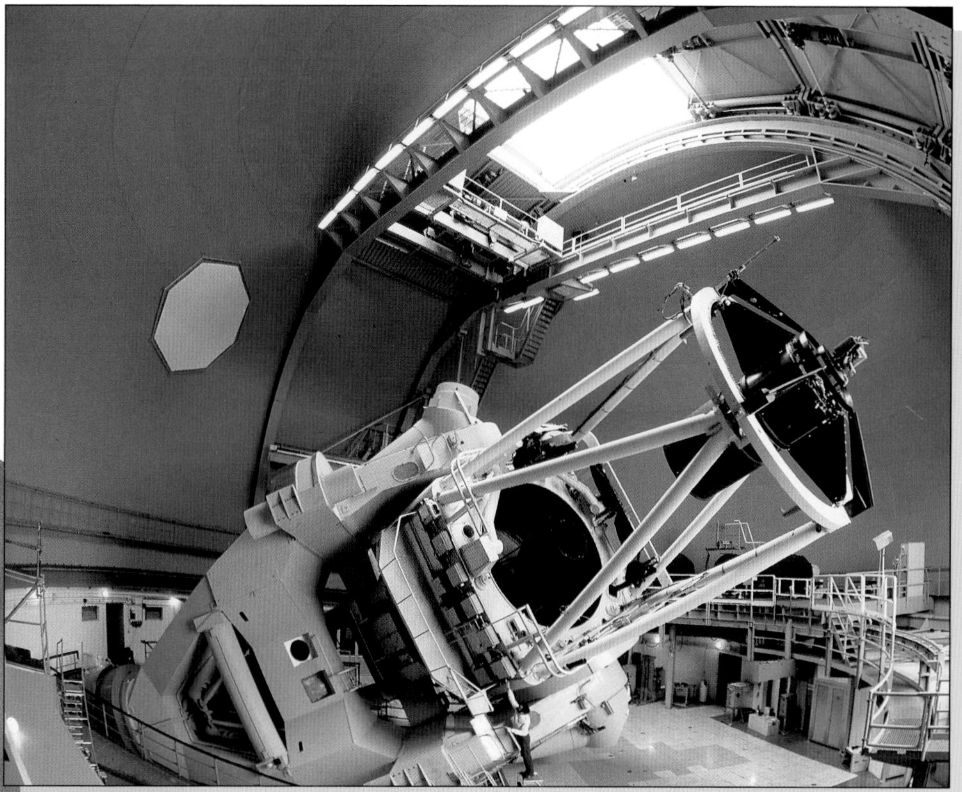

*Telescopes like this have shown astonomers that our solar system is part of a cluster of 100 billion stars, called a galaxy. There are millions of galaxies in the Universe.*

The Universe is a huge place. It is so big that scientists measure very big distances in light years - the distance light travels in a year, about 9,500,000,000,000 kilometres. Here are a few distances.

**Earth to Moon: 380,000 km**
**Earth to Sun: 150,000,000 km**
**Width of our solar system: 10,000,000,000 km**
**Distance to the next closest galaxy: 1,600,000,000,000,000,000 km**

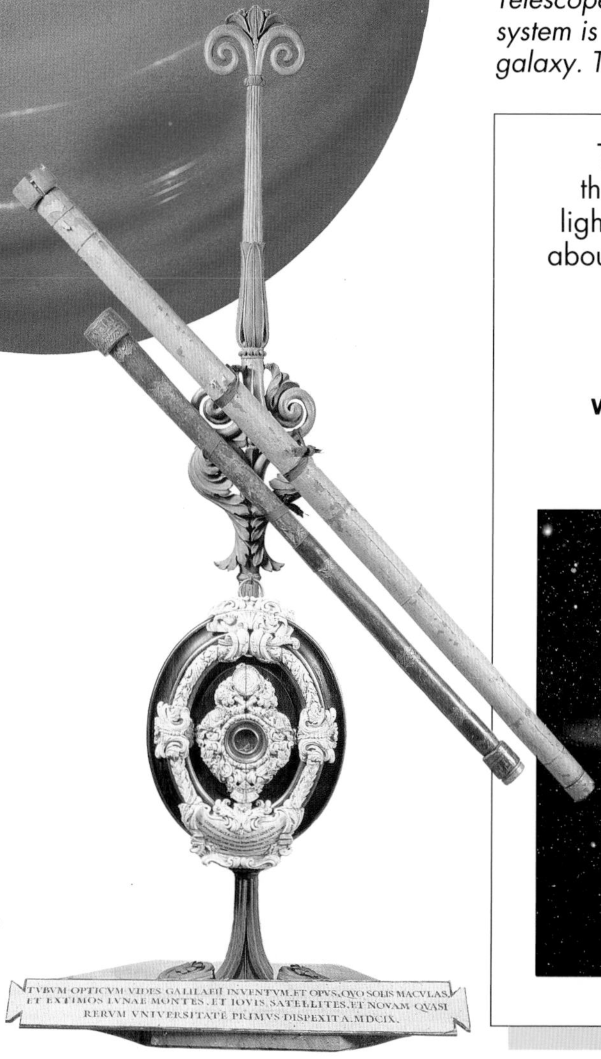
TVBVM OPTICVM VIDES GALILAEII INVENTVM.ET OPVS.QVO SOLIS MACVLAS.
ET EXTIMOS LVNAE MONTES. ET IOVIS SATELLITES.ET NOVAM QVASI
RERVM VNIVERSITATE PRIMVS DISPEXIT A.MDCIX.

*This is the type of telescope perfected by the Italian astronomer Galileo Galilei at the beginning of the 17th century. It enabled Galileo to make new discoveries about the solar system, the planets and moon orbiting our sun.*

# INTO SPACE

**At the same time as the science of astronomy was being developed, writers were speculating about what the stars and planets were like. The next stage was to actually go into space, and study them.**

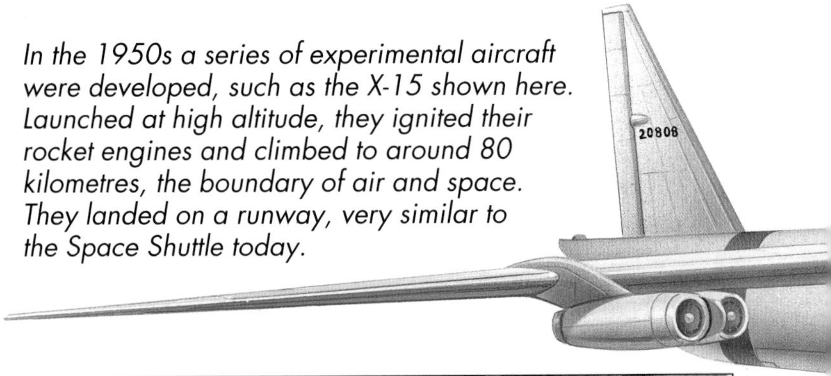

*In the 1950s a series of experimental aircraft were developed, such as the X-15 shown here. Launched at high altitude, they ignited their rocket engines and climbed to around 80 kilometres, the boundary of air and space. They landed on a runway, very similar to the Space Shuttle today.*

## ROCKETRY

In the 20th century, the new technology of rocketry was developed. In Russia, Konstantin Tsiolkovsky provided the theory of spaceflight and forecast the use of spacesuits, rockets and space stations half a century before the space age began. In Germany, Herman Oberth worked on the early theories of rockets and space travel. Then, in 1926, American Robert Goddard put theory into practice by launching the world's first successful liquid-fuelled rocket. These 'fathers of spaceflight' had showed the way for humans to escape the pull of the Earth's gravity and to travel beyond the Earth.

NATIONAL
U.S.ARMY AIR CORPS

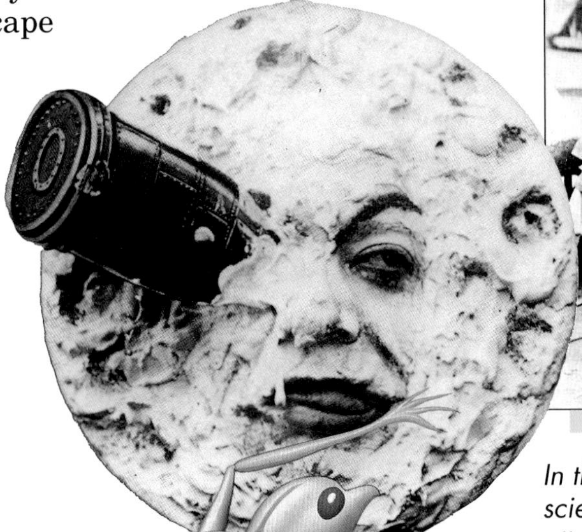

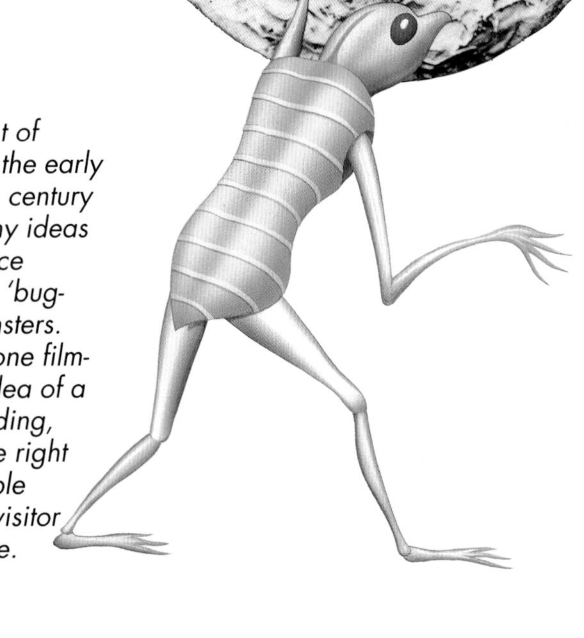

*The advent of cinema in the early half of this century led to many ideas about space travel and 'bug-eyed' monsters. Above is one film-maker's idea of a Moon landing, and on the right is a possible insectoid visitor from space.*

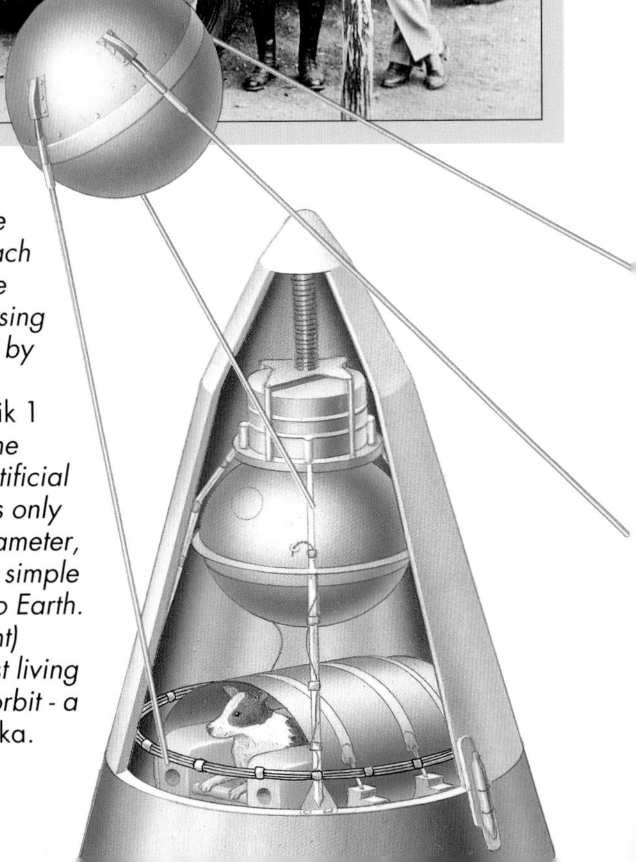

*In the 1930s, scientists made attempts to reach the limits of the atmosphere, using capsules lifted by balloons (top). Russia's Sputnik 1 (above) was the world's first artificial satellite. It was only 300 mm in diameter, but sent a few simple signals back to Earth. Sputnik 2 (right) carried the first living creature into orbit - a dog called Laika.*

## POSTWAR PROGRESS

During World War 2, Germany developed missile and rocket technology for military uses. After the war, many of the scientists continued their research in the Soviet Union and the USA. As a result, the Soviet Union launched its first Intercontinental Ballistic Missile (ICBM) in 1955. Then, on 4 October 1957, an ICBM was used to put *Sputnik 1*, the world's first satellite, into orbit (a circular path round the Earth). In America the Navy's *Vanguard* and the Army's *Explorer* competed to be the first US satellite. On 31 January 1958 *Explorer 1* was orbited. The space age was now a space race.

U.S AIR FORCE

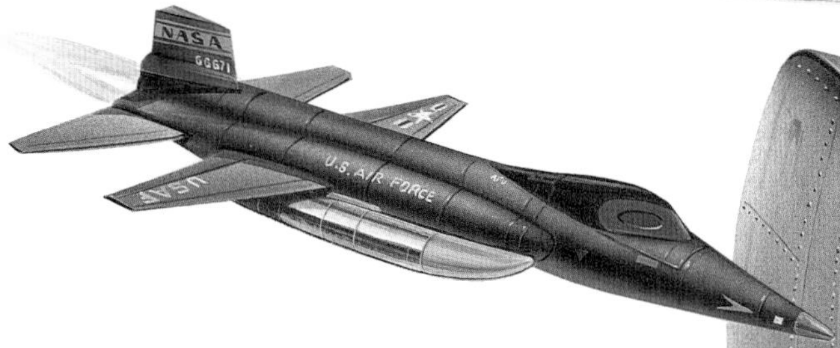
NASA

*American pioneer Robert Goddard stands by his historic liquid-fuelled rocket, first launched on 16 March 1926. Exactly 40 years later Neil Armstrong, the first human on the Moon, made his first spaceflight.*

*In the 19th century, writer Jules Verne described this 'Spacetrain'. Even then it was believed that journeys into space would become everyday events.*

# THE RIGHT STUFF

**On 12 April 1961 Soviet cosmonaut Yuri Gagarin became the first person in history to travel into space. He orbited the Earth once in 108 minutes in his spacecraft, *Vostok 1*, and began a new method of exploration - manned spaceflight.**

## SPACE EXPLORERS

Since then, over 300 people have flown in space. In the 1950s, no-one knew how the stress of launch, weightlessness and re-entry into the atmosphere would affect the human body. Therefore military aircraft test pilots were chosen to be the first space travellers. It was thought that their physical fitness, flying skill and experience of pushing high-performance aircraft to the very limits would enable them to withstand the stress of flying in a spacecraft.

## PIONEERS

These first astronauts were given a heroic image. They were pioneering space explorers risking their lives to increase our knowledge of space. Now that the effects of space travel are known, astronauts no longer need to be pilots but, rather, scientists. As space stations are built, the role of engineers, technicians and researchers becomes even more important. When bases are established on the Moon and Mars, astronauts will become builders, mining engineers and farmers, like the 19th century pioneers and 'homesteaders' of the American West.

LIBERTY
BELL
7

*This cosmonaut is on a multi-axial trainer, which will help him get used to the disorientation of spaceflight. Astronauts spend months practising every minute of the mission, following a timetable called a Flight Plan. There are also back-up astronauts ready in case a crew member is ill or injured.*

*The first astronauts had to be the right size to fit the spacecraft! For example, the Mercury capsule (above and right) was only 2.1m high - a very tight fit for an astronaut in a spacesuit.*

*The first person in space, Russian Yuri Gagarin (right), is shown in the cabin of* Vostok 1. Vostok 1 *orbited the Earth in a flight lasting 108 minutes.*

CCCP

*The US astronaut below is training for zero gravity in a special aircraft nicknamed the 'Vomit Comet'. The plane flies an up-and-down rollercoaster pattern, and at the top of the pattern the astronauts experience zero gravity.*

## WHAT QUALIFICATIONS?

Are you made of the 'Right Stuff' to be an astronaut? There is no age limit, but you must be mentally and physically fit, with a science degree. To be a pilot astronaut - qualified to fly the spacecraft - you must have 1,000 hours on high-performance jet aircraft. If you haven't got flying experience but have a scientific background you can still be a mission specialist, carrying out research. Other scientists can also train for a short time to carry out specialist research in space.

# TO THE MOON

**Even before the first satellites were put into space, there were plans to send machines called probes to the Moon and the planets. In 1961, US President Kennedy declared that an American would land on the Moon's surface before 1970.**

## FIRST PROBES

The Soviet effort to get there began well with its *Luna* probes. *Luna 2* sent back photos as it approached the Moon before crash-landing on the surface; then *Luna 9* made a soft landing and sent back 27 photos; and in September 1970 *Luna 16* returned with rock samples!

*Some ways to visit the Moon are shown in the diagram on the right. Many of the early missions did not even get beyond Earth orbit!*

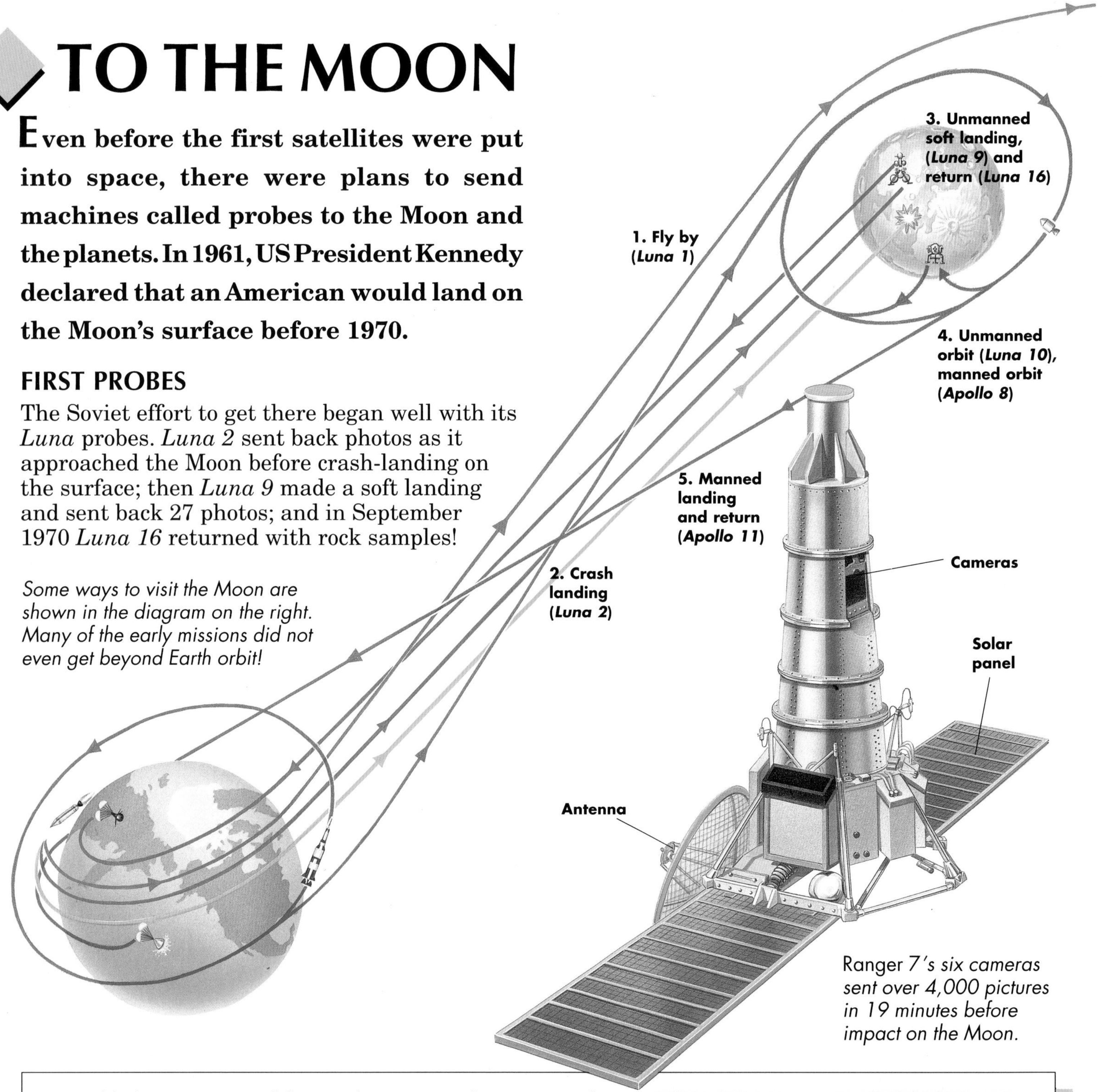

1. Fly by (Luna 1)
2. Crash landing (Luna 2)
3. Unmanned soft landing, (Luna 9) and return (Luna 16)
4. Unmanned orbit (Luna 10), manned orbit (Apollo 8)
5. Manned landing and return (Apollo 11)
Cameras
Solar panel
Antenna


*Ranger 7's six cameras sent over 4,000 pictures in 19 minutes before impact on the Moon.*

Listed below are some of the 80-plus unmanned missions to the Moon. *Surveyor 3* (right), which landed in April 1967, was visited by *Apollo 12's* astronauts in November 1969.

| | | | |
|---|---|---|---|
| ***Luna 1*** | **USSR** | **01/59** | **Flew by Moon** |
| ***Luna 2*** | **USSR** | **09/59** | **Crashlanded after taking photos** |
| ***Ranger 7*** | **USA** | **07/64** | **Sent back 4,300 photos** |
| ***Luna 9*** | **USSR** | **01/66** | **First soft landing** |
| ***Luna 10*** | **USSR** | **03/66** | **First probe to achieve lunar orbit** |
| ***Surveyor 1*** | **USA** | **05/66** | **Sent back 11,000 pictures** |
| ***Luna 13*** | **USSR** | **12/66** | **Tested soil** |
| ***Luna 16*** | **USSR** | **09/70** | **First automatic soil sample returned** |
| ***Luna 17*** | **USSR** | **11/70** | **First moon rover taken to surface** |
| ***Muses-A*** | **Japan** | **01/90** | **First to visit since 1976 (*Luna 24*)** |

## A GIANT STEP FOR MANKIND

However, the Americans had already gone one better. Despite their later start in the space race, they too had sent a number of probes to the Moon. Then, on 20 July 1969, the *Apollo 11* mission of Neil Armstrong and Edwin 'Buzz' Aldrin landed on the surface. While the world was watching this fabulous achievement, the third astronaut, Collins, was left to orbit the Moon in the Command Module. He even went out of radio contact with the Earth when he passed behind the Moon. Later *Apollo* astronauts gathered more samples, and drove a Lunar Rover over 15 km from the Lunar Module. In all, six *Apollo* missions landed on the Moon.

Apollo 9's *Command Module orbits Earth in March 1969. This photo was taken from the Lunar Module on its first test flight.*

**DID YOU KNOW?**

Spacecraft must be as light as possible. The lightweight ladder used by Neil Armstrong to climb down onto the Moon's surface could only take his weight because of the low gravity on the Moon. It would have broken under his real weight on Earth!

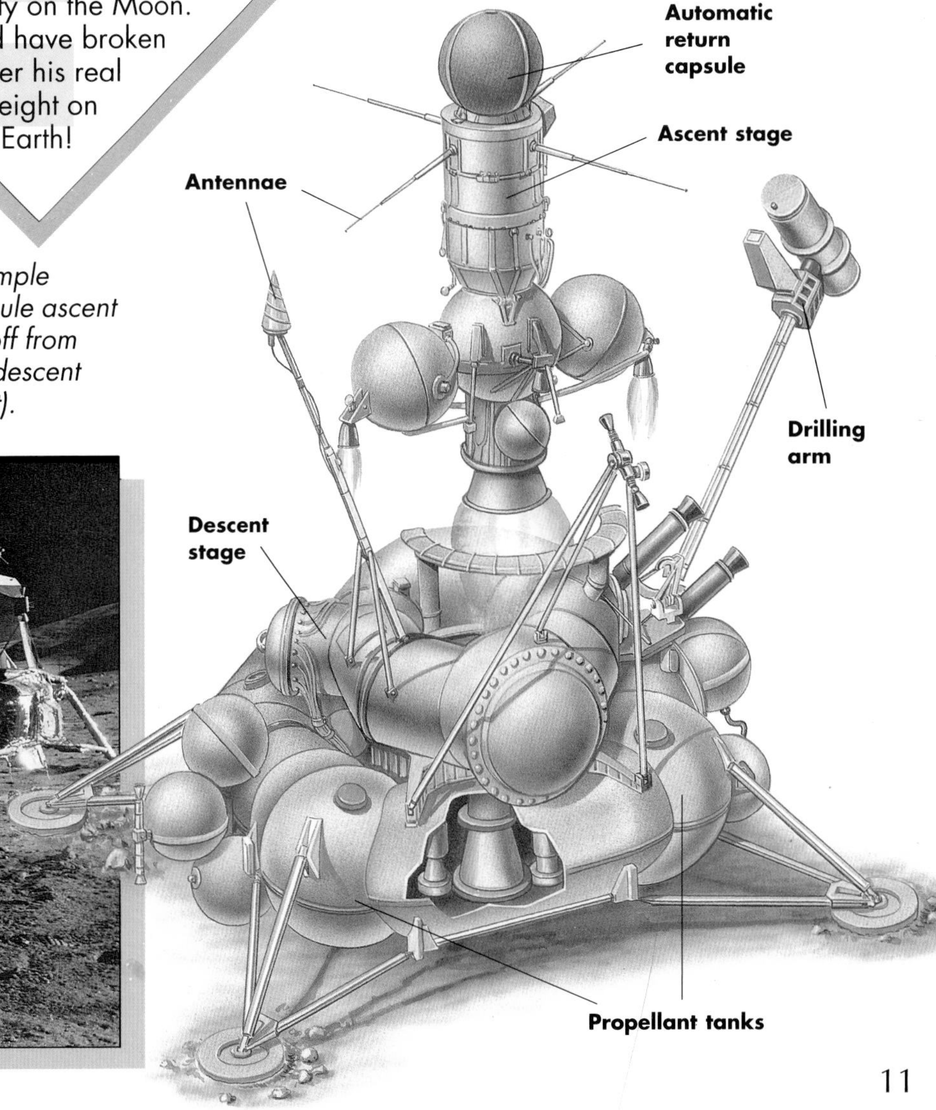
Automatic return capsule
Ascent stage
Antennae
Drilling arm
Descent stage
Propellant tanks

*The soil sample return capsule ascent stage lifts off from* Luna 16*'s descent stage (right).*

*Astronaut 'Jack' Schmitt stands with the Lunar Module* Challenger*, the Lunar Rover and the US flag during* Apollo 17*'s mission in 1972. This was the last of six* Apollo *landings.*

# LAUNCHERS

**The rocket, first used by the Chinese over 1,000 years ago, is the only practical way to enter space. It will remain the most efficient method of putting spacecraft into space for many years to come.**

## ROCKETS

Rockets work by burning fuel in the engines and letting it escape out of the exhausts. The thrust produced by this pushes the rocket in the opposite direction, rather like blowing up a toy balloon and letting it go to zoom around until all the air inside is used up. The larger the rocket, the more power it generates and the more weight it can carry.

*Here are some of the major launchers used in the space programme. The Saturn family of rockets was developed for the Apollo moon programme in the 1960s. Most of the 110-metre tall Saturn V rocket were the three huge stages needed to put the spacecraft on route to the Moon. Only the 3.9m tall Apollo Re-entry Module holding the three astronauts was recovered at the end of the mission.*

*Less power and fuel is needed when a rocket is lighter or when it travels faster. Therefore rockets are made up of sections. As each section's fuel is used up, the empty section is jettisoned to save weight (above).*

***Mercury-Atlas***

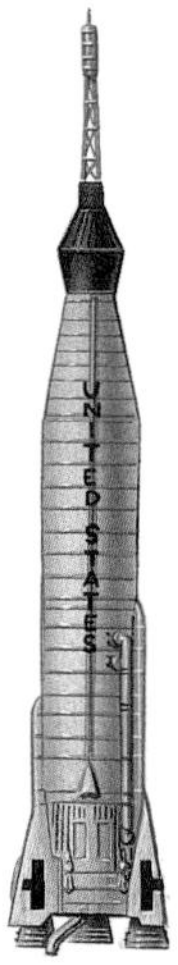
UNITED STATES

**1962-63**
**USA**

***Gemini-Titan***

**1965-66**
**USA**

***Soyuz SL-4***
**(*Rakyeta Nosityel Soyuz*)**

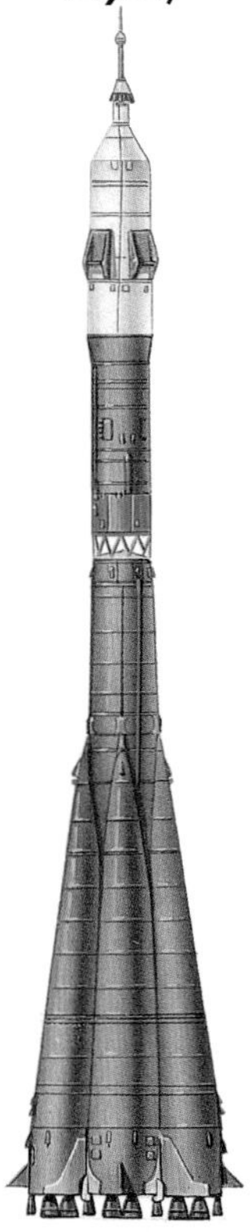

**1967 to date**
**USSR/Russia**

***Apollo-Saturn V***

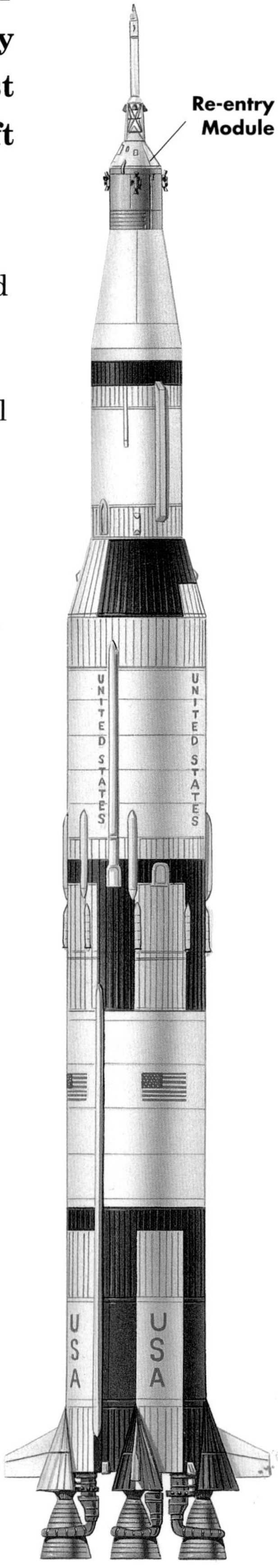
Re-entry Module
UNITED STATES
UNITED STATES
USA
USA

**1968-72**
**USA**

**Space Transportation System (Space Shuttle)**

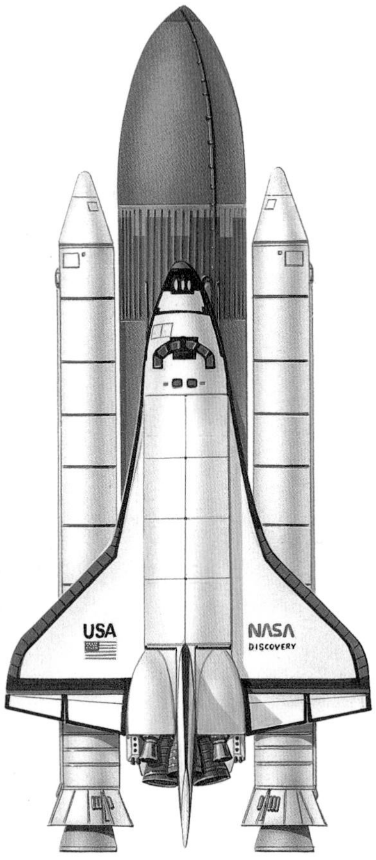
USA
NASA
DISCOVERY

**1981 to date**
**USA**

## A JOURNEY IN SPACE

Once launched, a spacecraft must be able to fly at about 30,000 kilometres per hour to escape the pull of gravity and stay in orbit - that's 100 times faster than the fastest racing car. If it flies too slowly, gravity will soon pull it back towards the Earth.

*Many countries still use ballistic rockets to put payloads into space. The European* Ariane *is one of these designs.*

esa
ariane

**DID YOU KNOW?**

Rocket fuel is very explosive, so it needs special storage. It has to be kept very cold so it does not evaporate away. If you could have sealed an ice cube in a *Saturn V* rocket tank, it would have taken eight years to melt!

## ROCKET POWER

To reach this velocity, a spacecraft needs a very powerful engine. The most common powerful engines are aeroplane jets, but even these are not powerful enough for spaceflight. Also, they need oxygen from air in order to work, and there isn't any air in space.

The only powerful engine that can work in space is a rocket, because it carries its own supply of oxygen as well as its fuel.

HLV
NASDA
H-II
NIPPON

*Japan, India and China have successful launchers. This artist's impression shows a Japanese H-II lift-off.*

## SHUTTLE SYSTEM

Every time a rocket is launched, very expensive equipment is lost. Most vehicles can only be used for one mission. However, the American Shuttle system was designed to be reusable, for mission after mission. The Shuttle Orbiter is launched by firing three main engines (fuelled from a massive External Tank) and two solid rocket boosters. Only the External Tank is lost; everything else can be recovered and reused.

# THE SPACE BASES

**Space missions begin months, sometimes years, before the moment of launch. All the preparations culminate with the hardware and crew coming together at the launch site, ready for lift-off.**

## KSC

Perhaps the most famous launch site is Kennedy Space Center (KSC) in the USA. Missions are launched out across the Atlantic away from heavily populated cities.

Yuri Gagarin was launched from the Baikonur Cosmodrome in Central Asia. This huge area, some 135 km by 90 km, covers several launch complexes and areas where the spacecraft are prepared for missions. All cosmonauts have taken off from here, as have several unmanned missions. They launch across the unpopulated deserts and steppes.

*The Space Shuttle* Atlantis *is moved to the launch pad at the Kennedy Space Center (above).*

*The major launch sites (below). Launches can be made into many different types of orbit.*

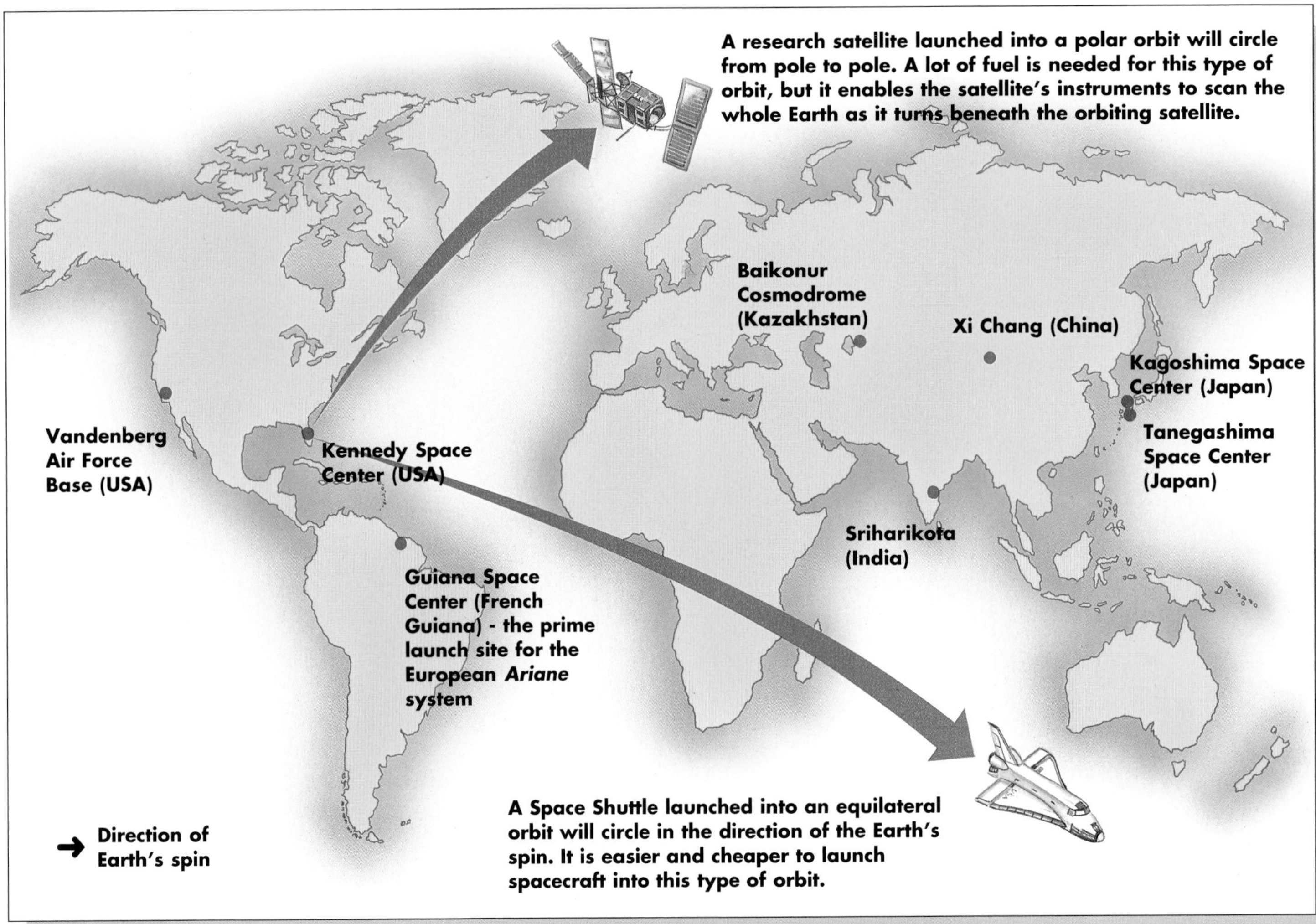
A research satellite launched into a polar orbit will circle from pole to pole. A lot of fuel is needed for this type of orbit, but it enables the satellite's instruments to scan the whole Earth as it turns beneath the orbiting satellite.
Baikonur Cosmodrome (Kazakhstan)
Xi Chang (China)
Kagoshima Space Center (Japan)
Tanegashima Space Center (Japan)
Vandenberg Air Force Base (USA)
Kennedy Space Center (USA)
Sriharikota (India)
Guiana Space Center (French Guiana) - the prime launch site for the European *Ariane* system
A Space Shuttle launched into an equilateral orbit will circle in the direction of the Earth's spin. It is easier and cheaper to launch spacecraft into this type of orbit.
Direction of Earth's spin

## STACKING

All sections of the mission launch vehicle are brought to KSC for checking before being assembled, or 'stacked', on the vehicle that will launch them. This is then taken to the pad for the launch. The whole mission is planned around a fixed deployment time or rendezvous.

*A Russian crew - actually two Russians and a Japanese cosmonaut - head for their awaiting Soyuz spacecraft. They will waddle, rather than walk, in their cumbersome spacesuits.*

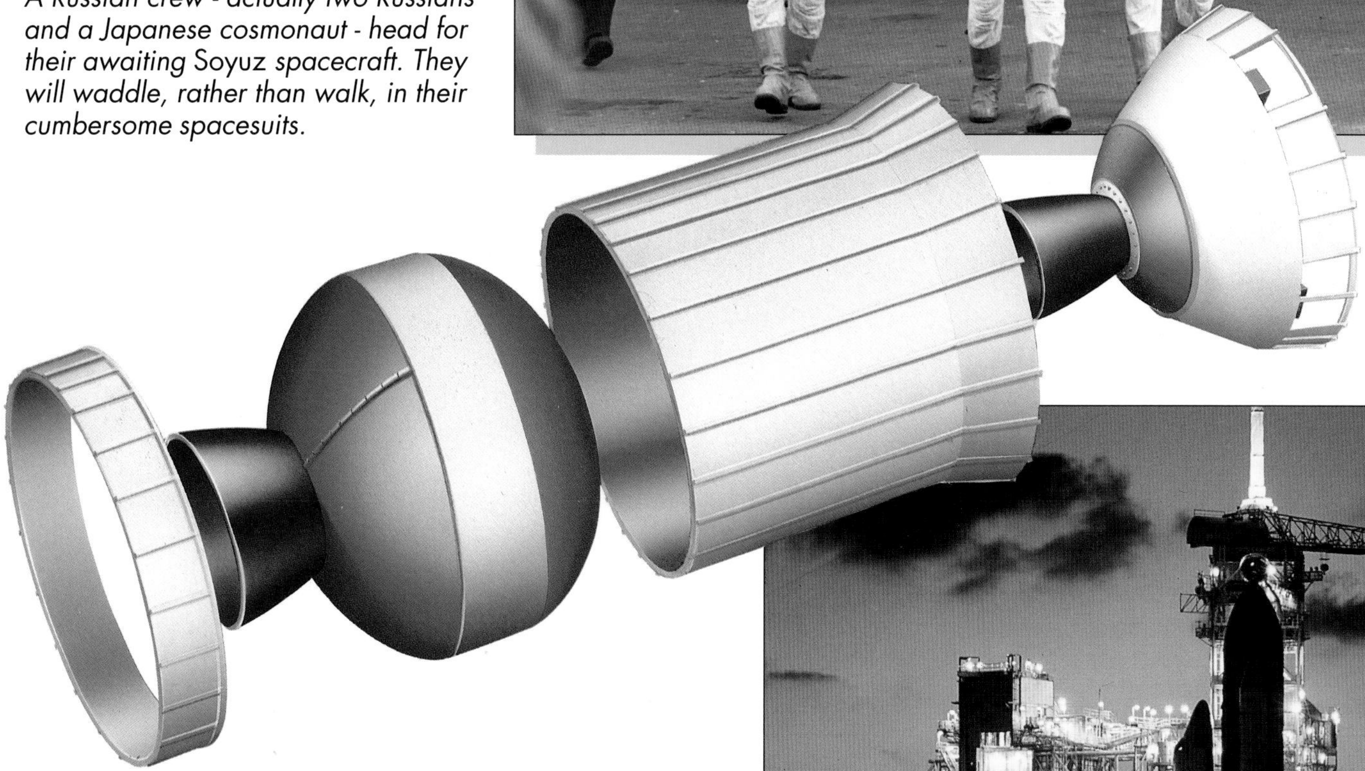

*Away from the launch pad, equipment is being assembled. These units will eventually boost a probe into deep space.*

*Even at night there's activity on the launch pad. Work continues around the clock to launch in time for a set rendezvous or deployment.*

## READY FOR LAUNCH

Once the vehicle is on the launch pad, hundreds of computers monitor and test every one of its systems. Fuel is loaded into the spacecraft and rocket from huge tanks around the pad, and finally the remaining payloads are put aboard. The crew usually board the vehicle about two hours before launch, support astronauts helping them strap into the vehicle. Then the hatches are sealed and the pad evacuated. The crew must now wait for launch.

# LIFT-OFF!

**The lift-off has always been the most dangerous part of any spaceflight. Sitting on top of thousands of litres of fuel is always a risky operation. There are thousands of things that have to work in sequence before the vehicle lifts off the pad.**

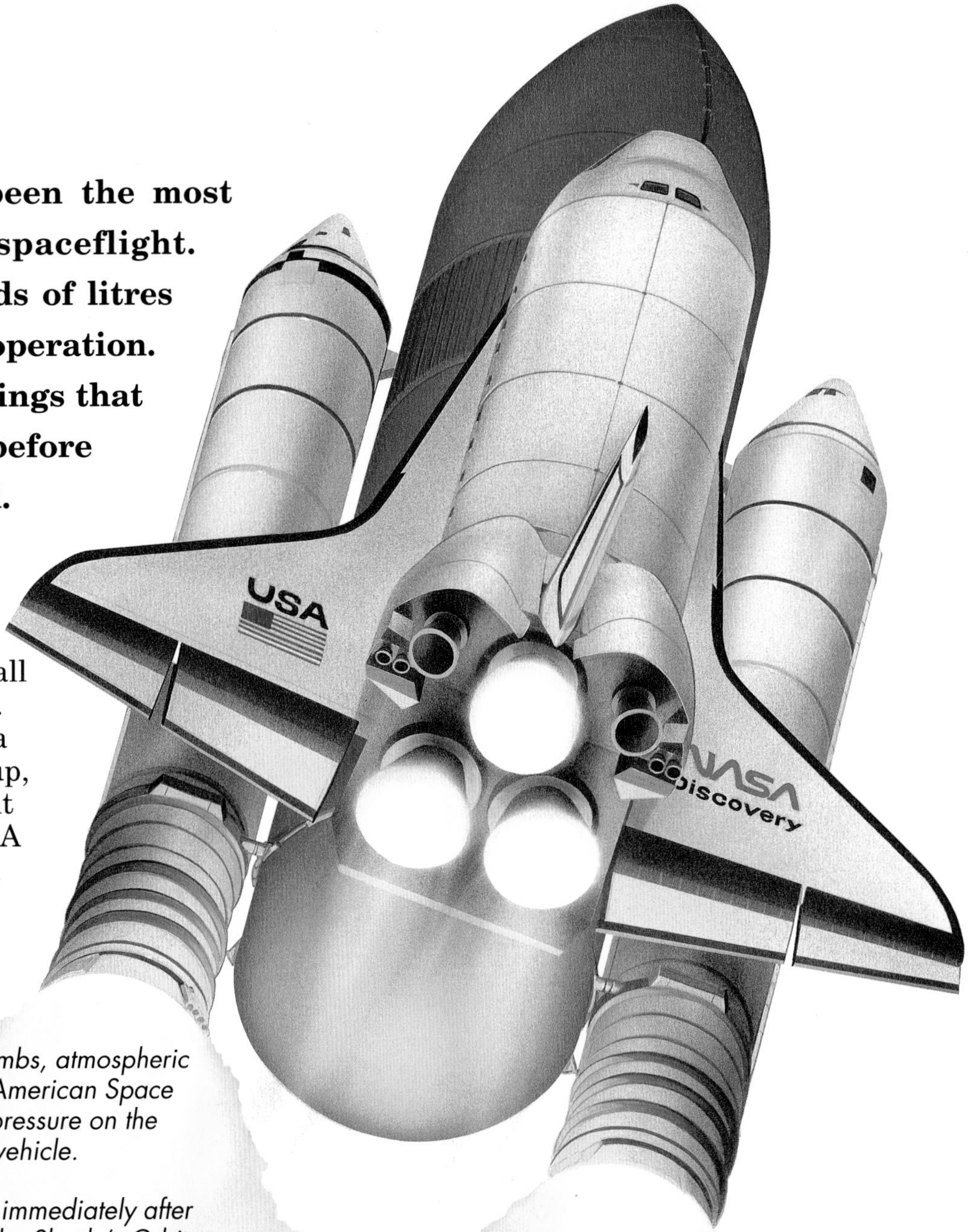
USA
NASA

## LAUNCH

Seconds before launch the computers tell the engines to ignite. They burst into life and all ground connections are severed. Clamps hold the spacecraft for a few seconds to let thrust build up, then they are released and flight begins. 'LIFT OFF...WE HAVE A LIFT OFF!' calls ground control as the vehicle clears the launch tower and heads for space.

*'TOWER CLEAR.' As the spacecraft climbs, atmospheric pressure on its surface increases. The American Space Shuttle rolls around 120° to ease this pressure on the Orbiter, the aeroplane-like part of the vehicle.*

*Preparations for the next launch begin immediately after touchdown. Below, a huge crane lifts the Shuttle's Orbiter onto a carrier aircraft. The Orbiter will be taken to KSC for a new cycle of ground processing, and its next lift-off.*

## 'GO AT THROTTLE UP'

As the vehicle climbs, empty stages are detached and the speed increases. As engines burn out and stages separate, a short lunge forward is experienced as the momentum of flight is briefly slowed, then a kick back into the seats as the new engines ignite.

## A BUMPY RIDE

There is not much the crew can do as computers tick away the planned sequence of events. Inside it's a very bumpy ride as the crew are pressed into their seats due to the G-forces of launch. Finally the spacecraft separates from the last stage and fires a small control jet to punch it into a safe Earth orbit 160 kilometres above the Earth. The most dangerous part of the mission is now over.

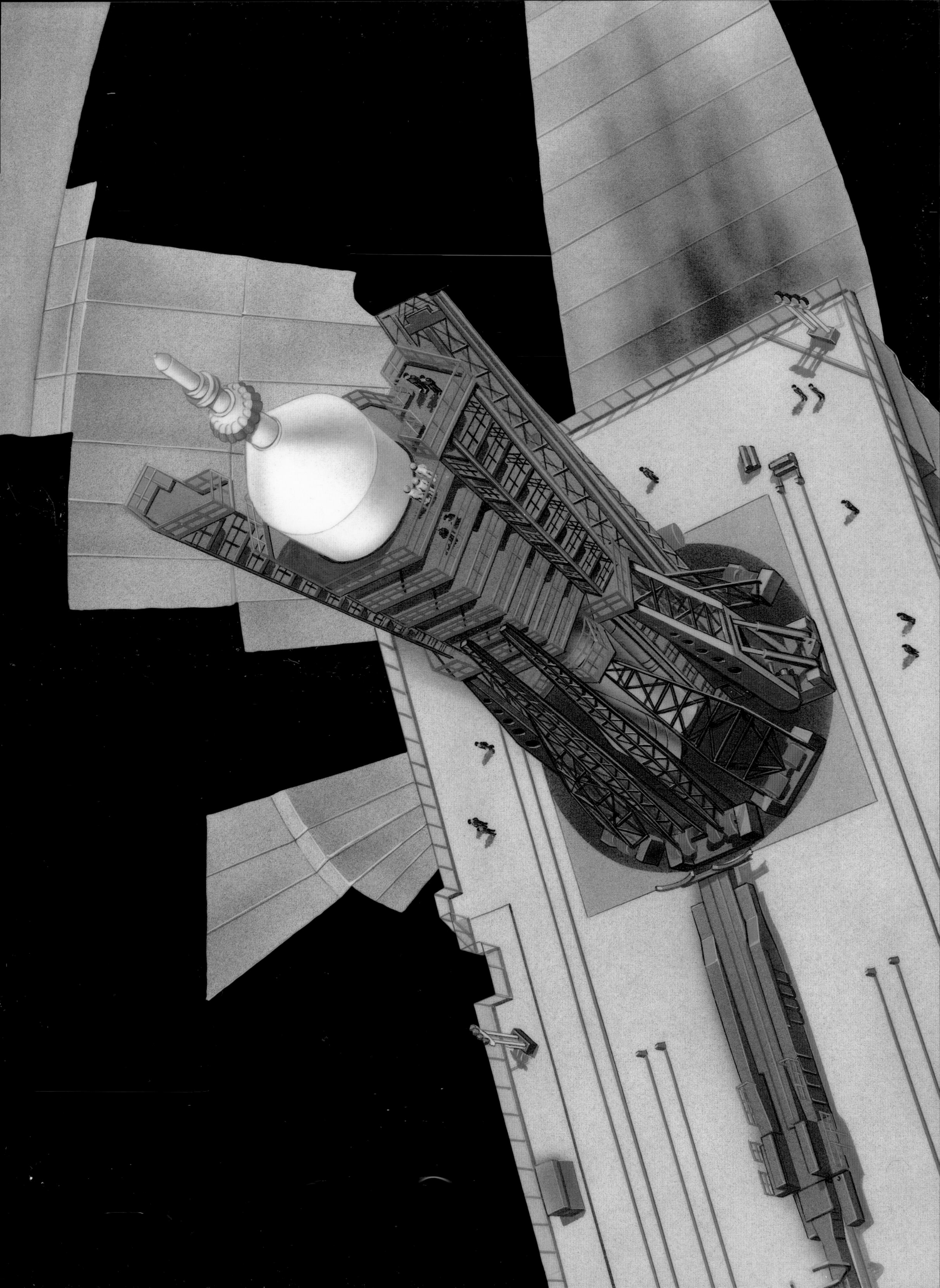

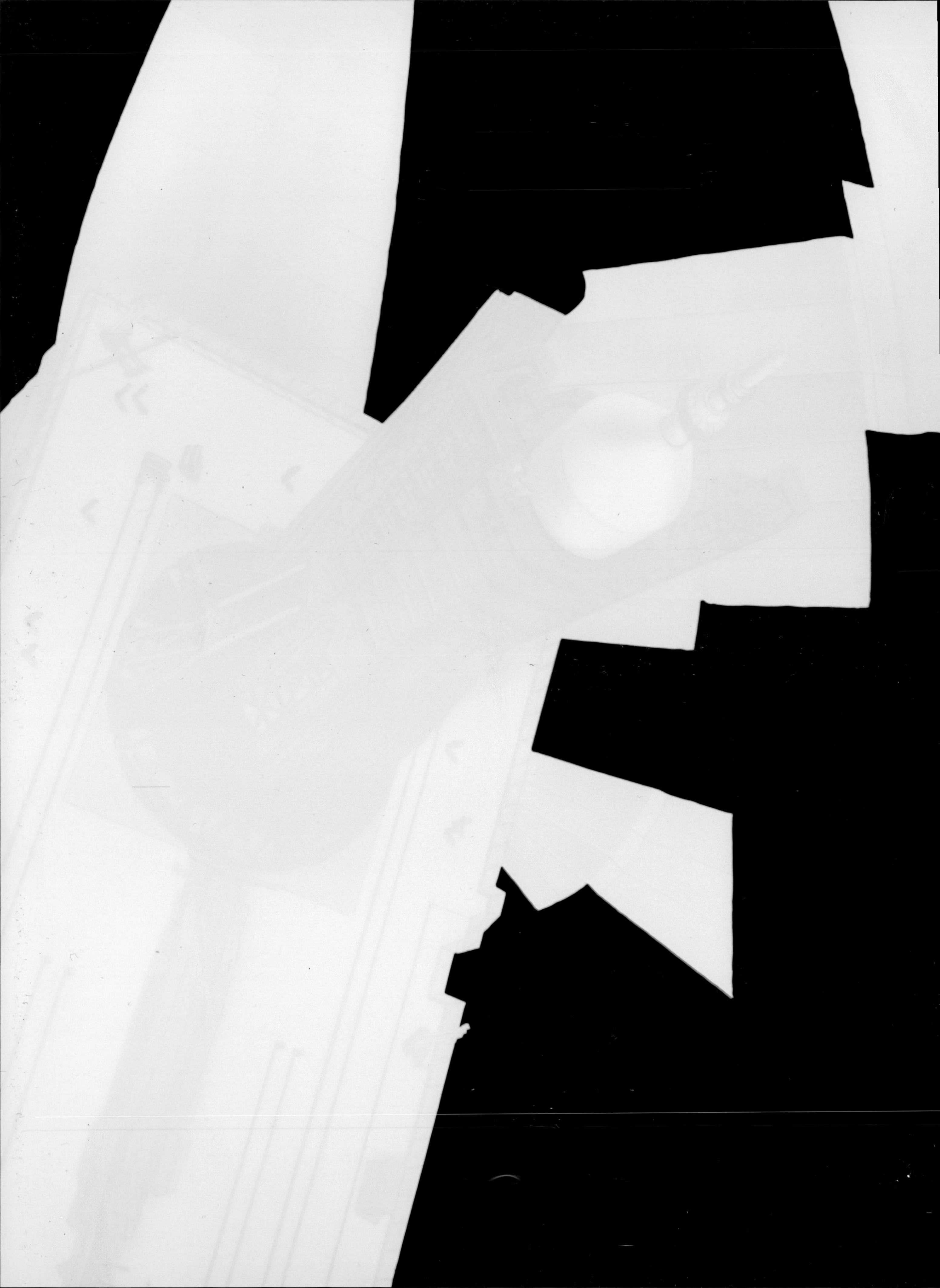

## A *SOYUZ* LAUNCH

The Russian SL-4 rocket first flew in 1955 and is still the main Russian launch system. Unlike the American method of vertical assembly, or stacking, of spacecraft, the Russians stack their launch vehicles horizontally, usually on railway carriages. These are taken to the launch pad and the rocket is raised vertically. At launch the rocket exhausts are directed away into a huge canyon. Countdown is very automated, and launch always occurs on time - in contrast to the many delays and aborts of US launches.

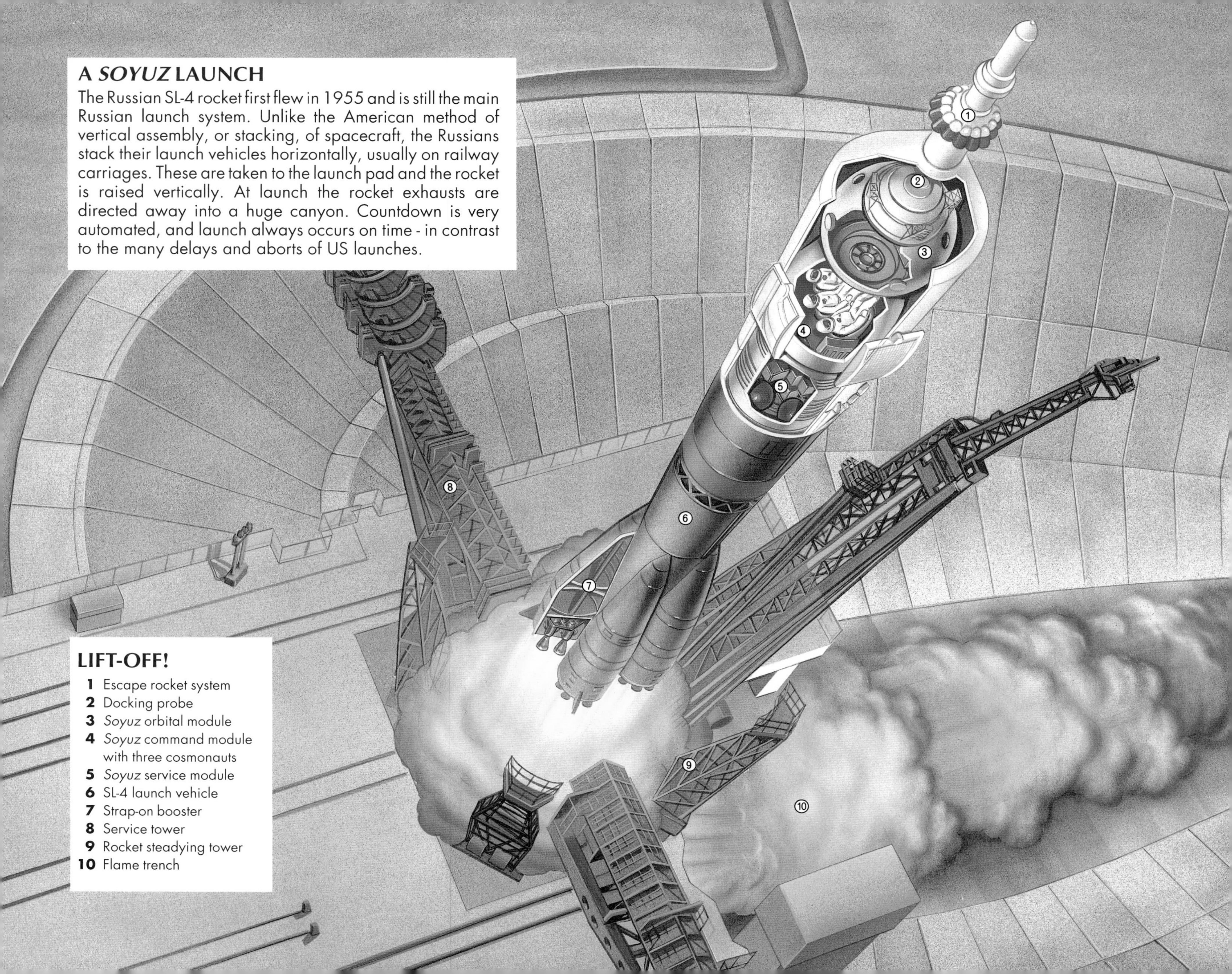
1
2
3
4
5
6
7
8
9
10

## LIFT-OFF!

**1** Escape rocket system
**2** Docking probe
**3** *Soyuz* orbital module
**4** *Soyuz* command module with three cosmonauts
**5** *Soyuz* service module
**6** SL-4 launch vehicle
**7** Strap-on booster
**8** Service tower
**9** Rocket steadying tower
**10** Flame trench

# A JOURNEY THROUGH SPACE

**Every spacecraft is launched to perform a mission. This might be to deploy a satellite, to rendezvous (meet up) with another spacecraft, or to visit a distant planet. Scientists must calculate the launch time and flight-path of the mission very carefully.**

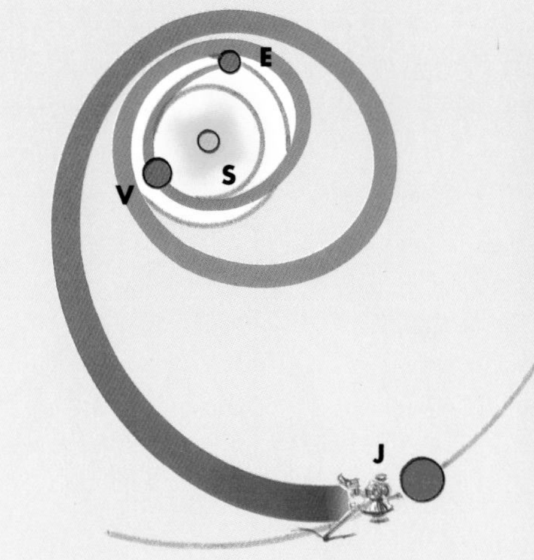
E
S
V
J

The *Galileo* space probe was launched towards the Sun (**S**). It used the gravity of Venus (**V**) and the Earth (**E**) to propel it like a sling shot on its six-year journey to Jupiter (**J**).

## RIGHT TIME, RIGHT PATH

The Earth, the planets and other spacecraft are all moving around in space. Therefore there are only certain times, called launch windows, when a spacecraft can be launched to meet up with its target. If a launch misses its window, it must wait for another one, which may be days or even months away.

Once in space, the spacecraft must be navigated. On the Space Shuttle, for example, the crew take visual sightings of certain stars and planets. The Shuttle's computer compares these sightings with its own record of star positions, and calculates the Shuttle's true position.

## A HELPING HAND

The space probe *Galileo* was launched on a mission to Jupiter. It was taken into space by the Space Shuttle, then fired on its way by a special booster. Once the booster had used up its fuel, it was jettisoned, leaving *Galileo* to continue with just enough fuel for manoeuvring.

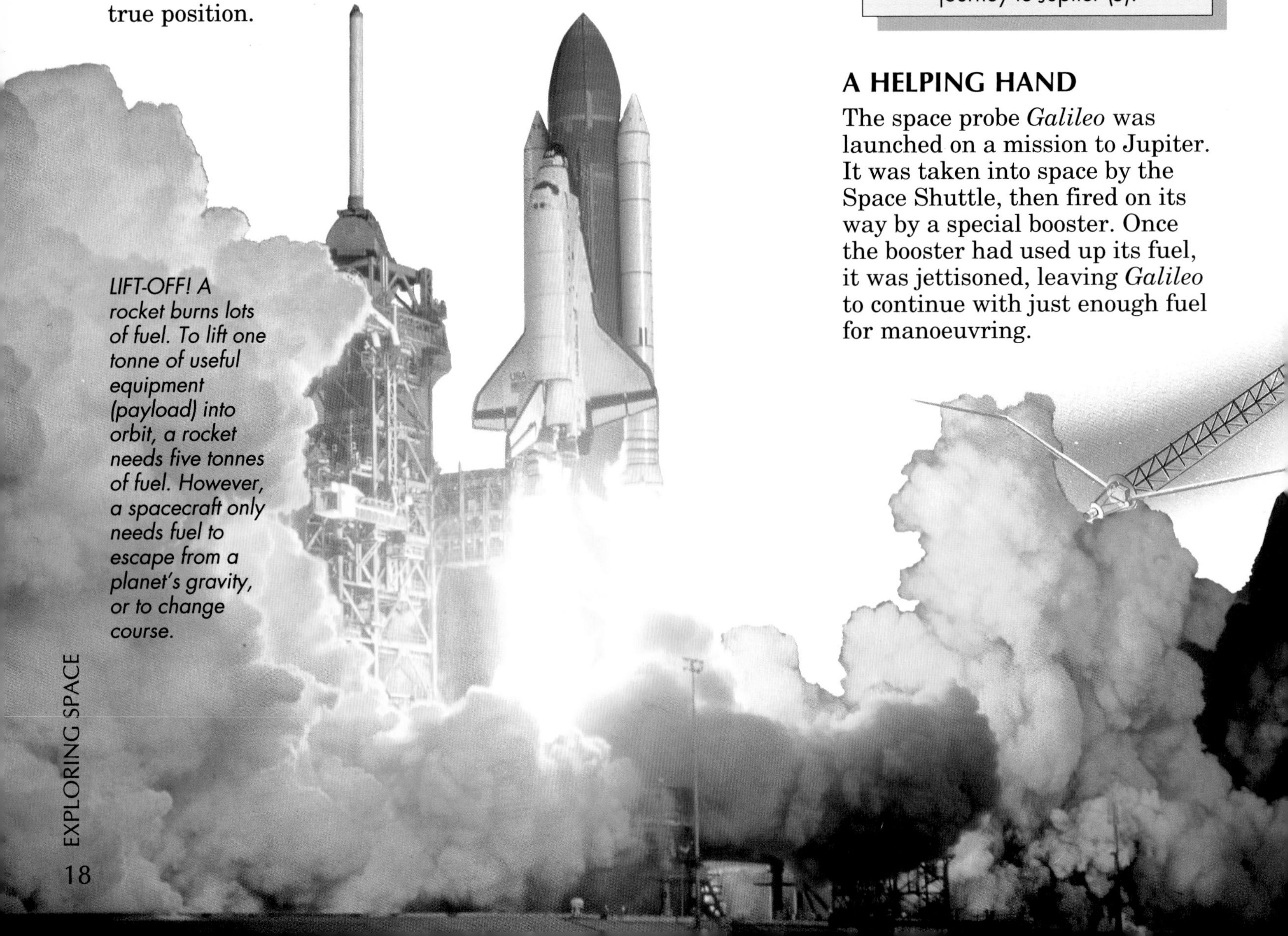

*LIFT-OFF! A rocket burns lots of fuel. To lift one tonne of useful equipment (payload) into orbit, a rocket needs five tonnes of fuel. However, a spacecraft only needs fuel to escape from a planet's gravity, or to change course.*

## SLING SHOT

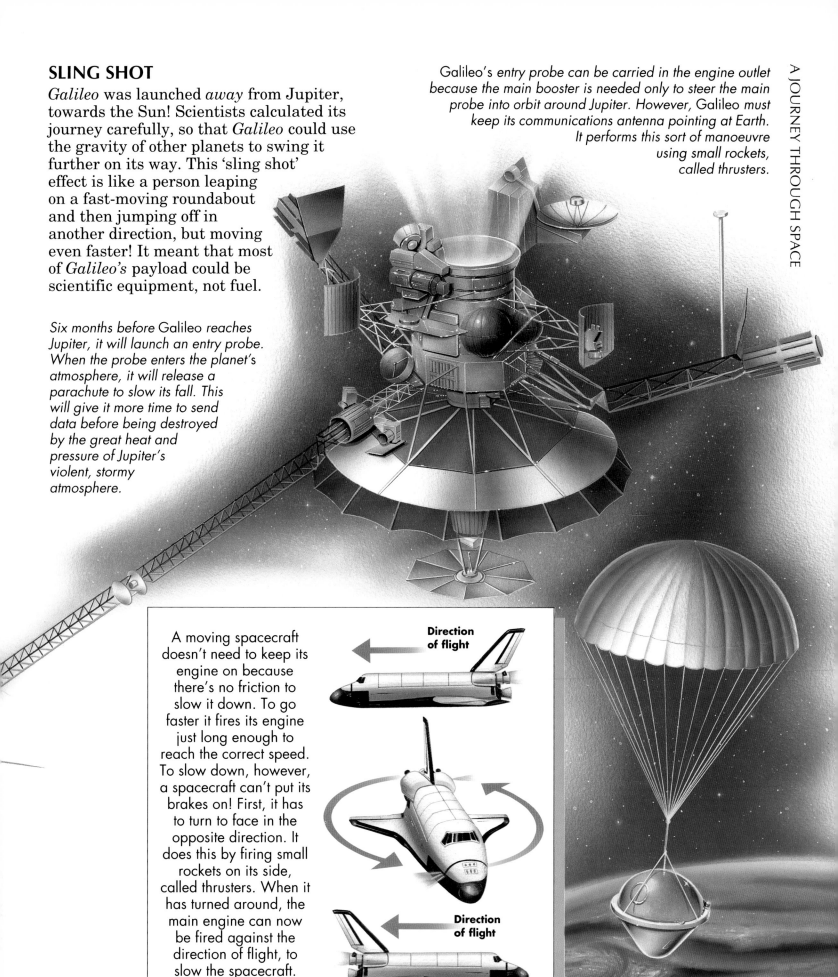

*Galileo* was launched *away* from Jupiter, towards the Sun! Scientists calculated its journey carefully, so that *Galileo* could use the gravity of other planets to swing it further on its way. This 'sling shot' effect is like a person leaping on a fast-moving roundabout and then jumping off in another direction, but moving even faster! It meant that most of *Galileo's* payload could be scientific equipment, not fuel.

*Galileo's entry probe can be carried in the engine outlet because the main booster is needed only to steer the main probe into orbit around Jupiter. However, Galileo must keep its communications antenna pointing at Earth. It performs this sort of manoeuvre using small rockets, called thrusters.*

*Six months before* Galileo *reaches Jupiter, it will launch an entry probe. When the probe enters the planet's atmosphere, it will release a parachute to slow its fall. This will give it more time to send data before being destroyed by the great heat and pressure of Jupiter's violent, stormy atmosphere.*

A moving spacecraft doesn't need to keep its engine on because there's no friction to slow it down. To go faster it fires its engine just long enough to reach the correct speed. To slow down, however, a spacecraft can't put its brakes on! First, it has to turn to face in the opposite direction. It does this by firing small rockets on its side, called thrusters. When it has turned around, the main engine can now be fired against the direction of flight, to slow the spacecraft.

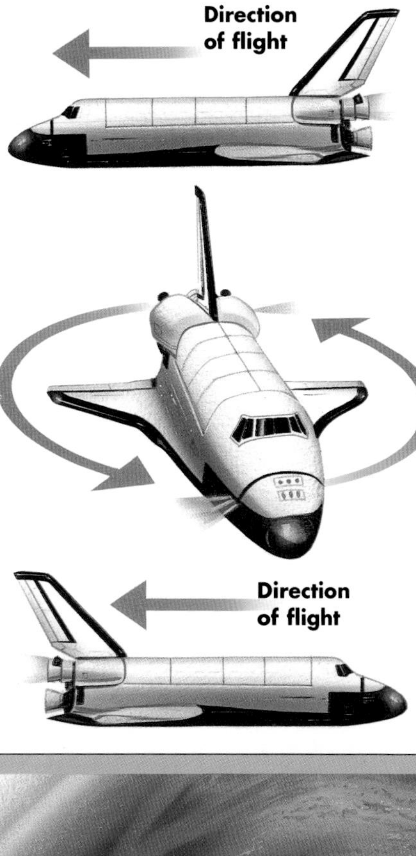
Direction of flight
Direction of flight

# RETURN TO EARTH

**Returning to Earth is nearly as difficult as take-off. The re-entry module has to fly through the atmosphere. At the high speed of space-flight, this generates very high temperatures on the outside of the spacecraft.**

Survival courses prepare astronauts for emergencies. In 1965, two cosmonauts spent 24 hours waiting for the rescue team. They had to light fires to keep wolves away!

## RESISTING THE HEAT

At the end of the mission, the crew fire the engines against the direction of flight to slow it down. They then separate the re-entry module from the rest of the spacecraft and turn it to point the heat shield towards the direction of flight, to take most of the high temperatures. The capsule is also designed to use the atmosphere as a brake as it falls back to Earth.

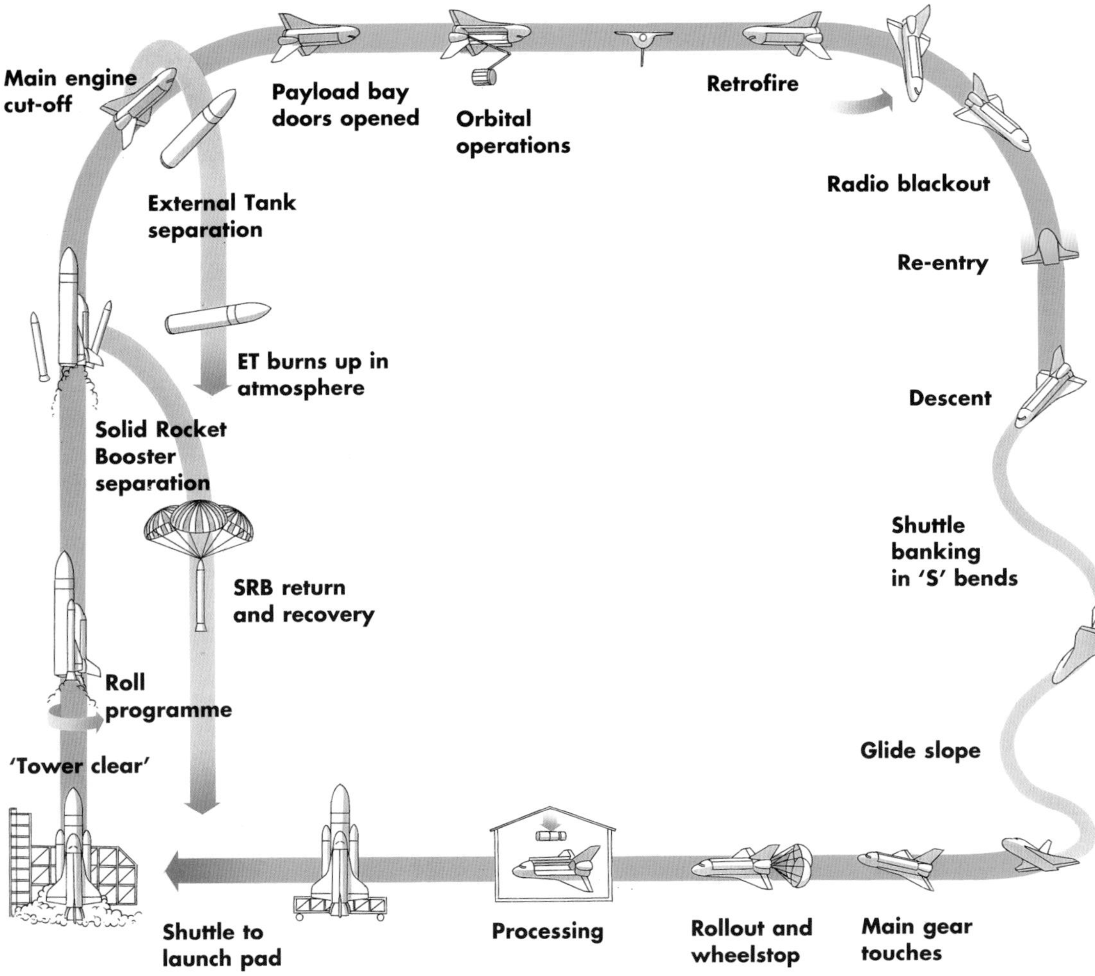
Main engine cut-off
Payload bay doors opened
Orbital operations
Retrofire
Radio blackout
Re-entry
External Tank separation
ET burns up in atmosphere
Descent
Solid Rocket Booster separation
Shuttle banking in 'S' bends
SRB return and recovery
Roll programme
'Tower clear'
Glide slope
Shuttle to launch pad
Processing
Rollout and wheelstop
Main gear touches

*The diagram on the left shows a typical NASA Space Shuttle mission profile, from countdown to touchdown and processing for the next mission. The Shuttle takes off from Kennedy Space Center, and ideally lands back there. Sometimes, for safety reasons, a landing is made in California. Then the Orbiter has to be flown to KSC on a carrier aircraft (see page 16).*

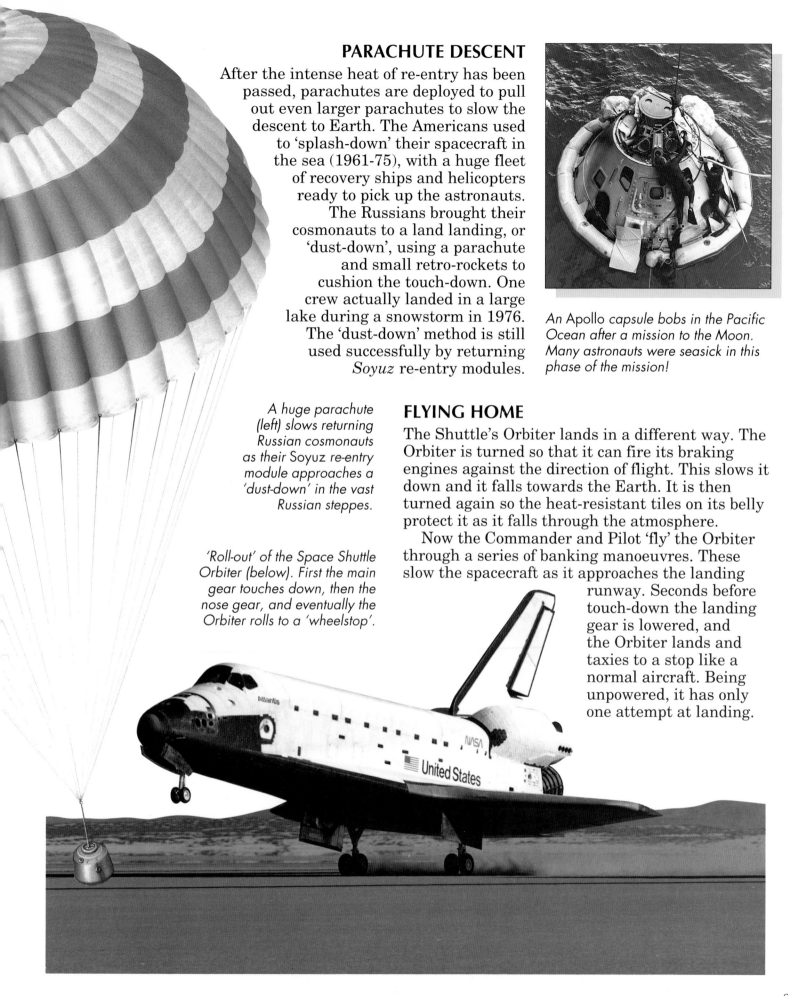

## PARACHUTE DESCENT

After the intense heat of re-entry has been passed, parachutes are deployed to pull out even larger parachutes to slow the descent to Earth. The Americans used to 'splash-down' their spacecraft in the sea (1961-75), with a huge fleet of recovery ships and helicopters ready to pick up the astronauts.

The Russians brought their cosmonauts to a land landing, or 'dust-down', using a parachute and small retro-rockets to cushion the touch-down. One crew actually landed in a large lake during a snowstorm in 1976. The 'dust-down' method is still used successfully by returning *Soyuz* re-entry modules.

*An Apollo capsule bobs in the Pacific Ocean after a mission to the Moon. Many astronauts were seasick in this phase of the mission!*

*A huge parachute (left) slows returning Russian cosmonauts as their Soyuz re-entry module approaches a 'dust-down' in the vast Russian steppes.*

## FLYING HOME

The Shuttle's Orbiter lands in a different way. The Orbiter is turned so that it can fire its braking engines against the direction of flight. This slows it down and it falls towards the Earth. It is then turned again so the heat-resistant tiles on its belly protect it as it falls through the atmosphere.

Now the Commander and Pilot 'fly' the Orbiter through a series of banking manoeuvres. These slow the spacecraft as it approaches the landing runway. Seconds before touch-down the landing gear is lowered, and the Orbiter lands and taxies to a stop like a normal aircraft. Being unpowered, it has only one attempt at landing.

*'Roll-out' of the Space Shuttle Orbiter (below). First the main gear touches down, then the nose gear, and eventually the Orbiter rolls to a 'wheelstop'.*

Atlantis
NASA
United States

# GROUND CONTROL

**All missions need the support of scientists, engineers and technicians on Earth. The most famous are NASA's Mission Control Center in Houston, Texas, used for all American manned spaceflights, and the Jet Propulsion Laboratory in California, used for unmanned missions. In Russia a huge centre near Moscow controls the *Mir* space station.**

## MISSION CONTROL

In mission control, shifts of flight controllers monitor the mission around the clock. They check that the spacecraft is on the right course. They make sure that communications links are working, and check that oxygen and fuel are not being used up too quickly. A fellow astronaut ('CapCom') provides a link between the crew and the mission control team. In overall charge of flight control is a Flight Director, 'Flight', who is responsible for the safety and success of the mission and crew.

*A Chinese mission control room. It seems very sparsely manned, compared to Russian and American mission controls.*

## DEEP SPACE

A less complex mission control is used for deep space probes, as there's no crew to talk to. Good communications are essential for deep space missions, because of the long distances to the spacecraft (it's nearly 100 million kilometres to Mars, for example). Signals must be focussed very accurately at the spacecraft's antenna so that the electronic signals are received clearly. There are often many minutes of 'silence' as the signal is travelling.

*Messages (right) are sent from the ground to a spacecraft via the TDRS (Tracking & Data Relay Satellites). The TDRS ground station communicates using two main 'bands' of electronic signals. The K band can send a lot of data very quickly, but its beam is not very easy to aim. The S band can't handle as much data, but its beam can be focused very accurately onto the antenna of a distant spacecraft.*

***GALILEO* SPACE PROBE**
***'Dit-dit-dit-dit-dit'*** **(digital data being transmitted to JPL Mission Control).**
**HUBBLE SPACE TELESCOPE**
**5. *'Blip blip, blip blip blip'*** **(signals being transmitted to user station).**
**DOMESTIC RELAY SATELLITE (DOMSAT)**
**JET PROPULSION LABORATORY, CALIFORNIA**
**MISSION CONTROL, HOUSTON, TEXAS**
**1. *'Discovery, this is Houston. Go for deploy.'***
**WHITE SANDS TRACKING STATION, NEW MEXICO**
**4. *'Houston - White Sands here. Signals received.'***

## DID YOU KNOW?

The design of computer on the Shuttle dates from the 1970s, and has only 480 kilobytes of Random Access Memory. (A modern home computer may have more than 2,000 kilobytes of RAM.) Many of the programs used on the mission are stored on tape and loaded into the main memory only when they are needed!

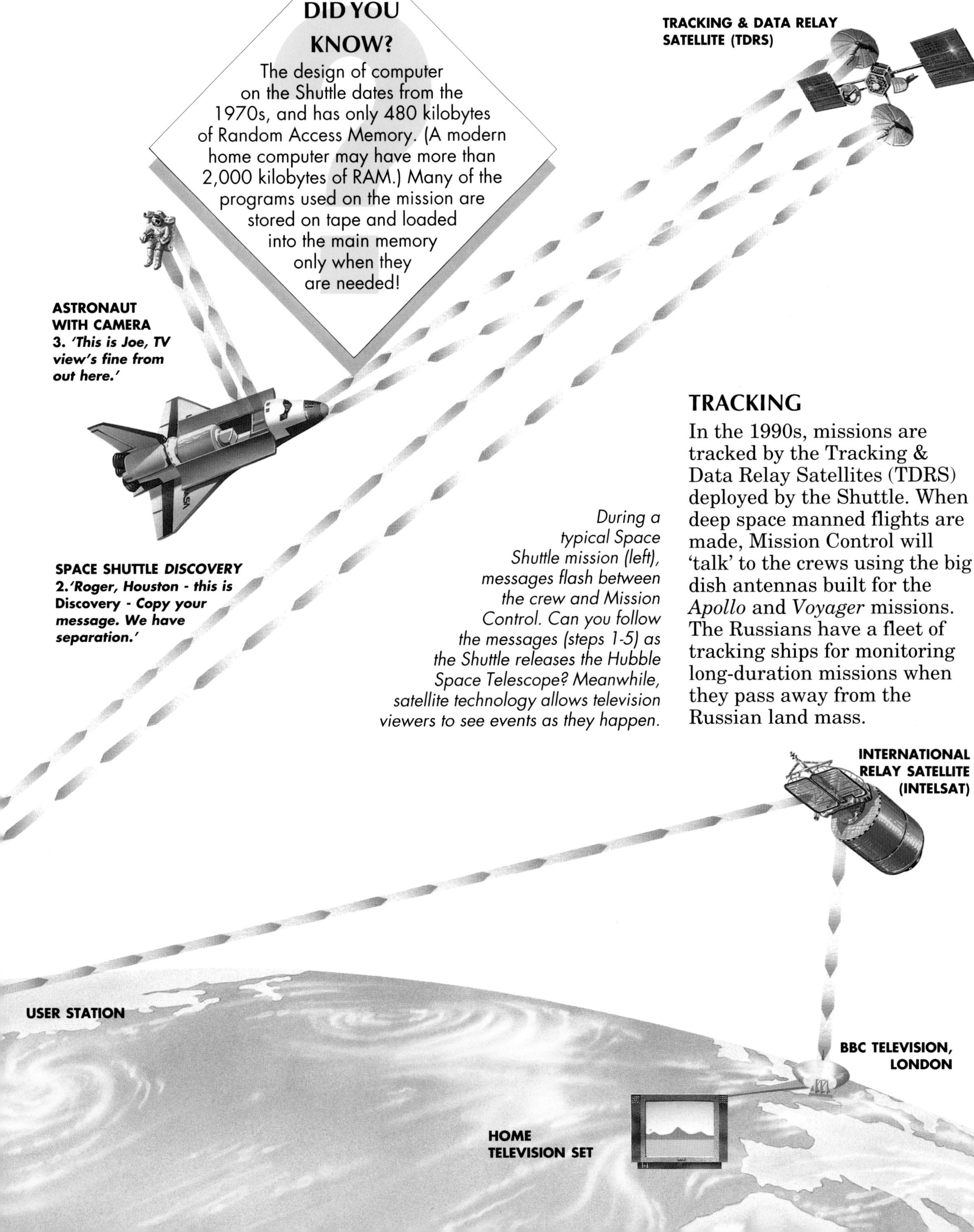
TRACKING & DATA RELAY SATELLITE (TDRS)
ASTRONAUT WITH CAMERA
3. 'This is Joe, TV view's fine from out here.'
SPACE SHUTTLE DISCOVERY
2.'Roger, Houston - this is Discovery - Copy your message. We have separation.'
INTERNATIONAL RELAY SATELLITE (INTELSAT)
USER STATION
BBC TELEVISION, LONDON
HOME TELEVISION SET

*During a typical Space Shuttle mission (left), messages flash between the crew and Mission Control. Can you follow the messages (steps 1-5) as the Shuttle releases the Hubble Space Telescope? Meanwhile, satellite technology allows television viewers to see events as they happen.*

## TRACKING

In the 1990s, missions are tracked by the Tracking & Data Relay Satellites (TDRS) deployed by the Shuttle. When deep space manned flights are made, Mission Control will 'talk' to the crews using the big dish antennas built for the *Apollo* and *Voyager* missions. The Russians have a fleet of tracking ships for monitoring long-duration missions when they pass away from the Russian land mass.

# SPACE SHUTTLE

**Today, the most frequently used method of getting into space is the NASA Space Shuttle. The Shuttle is launched like a rocket, flies like a spacecraft and lands like a plane. It is a space truck, taking astronauts, cargo and experiments into space, and returning satellites and equipment to Earth. The vehicle can be reused, flying many missions into Earth orbit.**

*Coming home. The intense heat seems to fold around the Orbiter's nose.*

Columbia

## ENGINES AND BOOSTERS

The main part of the Space Shuttle 'stack' is the Orbiter. It has three powerful main engines fuelled from a large external tank. The External Tank (ET) is a huge fuel tank carrying gallons of liquid hydrogen and liquid oxygen. These are mixed and ignited in the main engines to push the vehicle into space. After eight minutes the ET is empty and discarded.

Two Solid Rocket Boosters (SRBs) help launch the Shuttle. Once ignited they cannot be stopped until the solid fuel, a kind of sludge, is used up after about two minutes.

## THE ORBITER

Shaped like an aircraft, the Orbiter carries the crew and payload to and from space. It has wings and a tail for the landing phase of the mission. Manoeuvring engines are located around the Orbiter. These can be fired to change the Orbiter's position in orbit.

*As the Shuttle heads into orbit, its scorched External Tank falls toward Earth. The ET, which is not reusable, will burn up in the Earth's atmosphere.*

*On the flightdeck in the 1980s. The myriad controls of the 1970s-designed Shuttle are now supplemented by lap-top computers and head-up displays.*

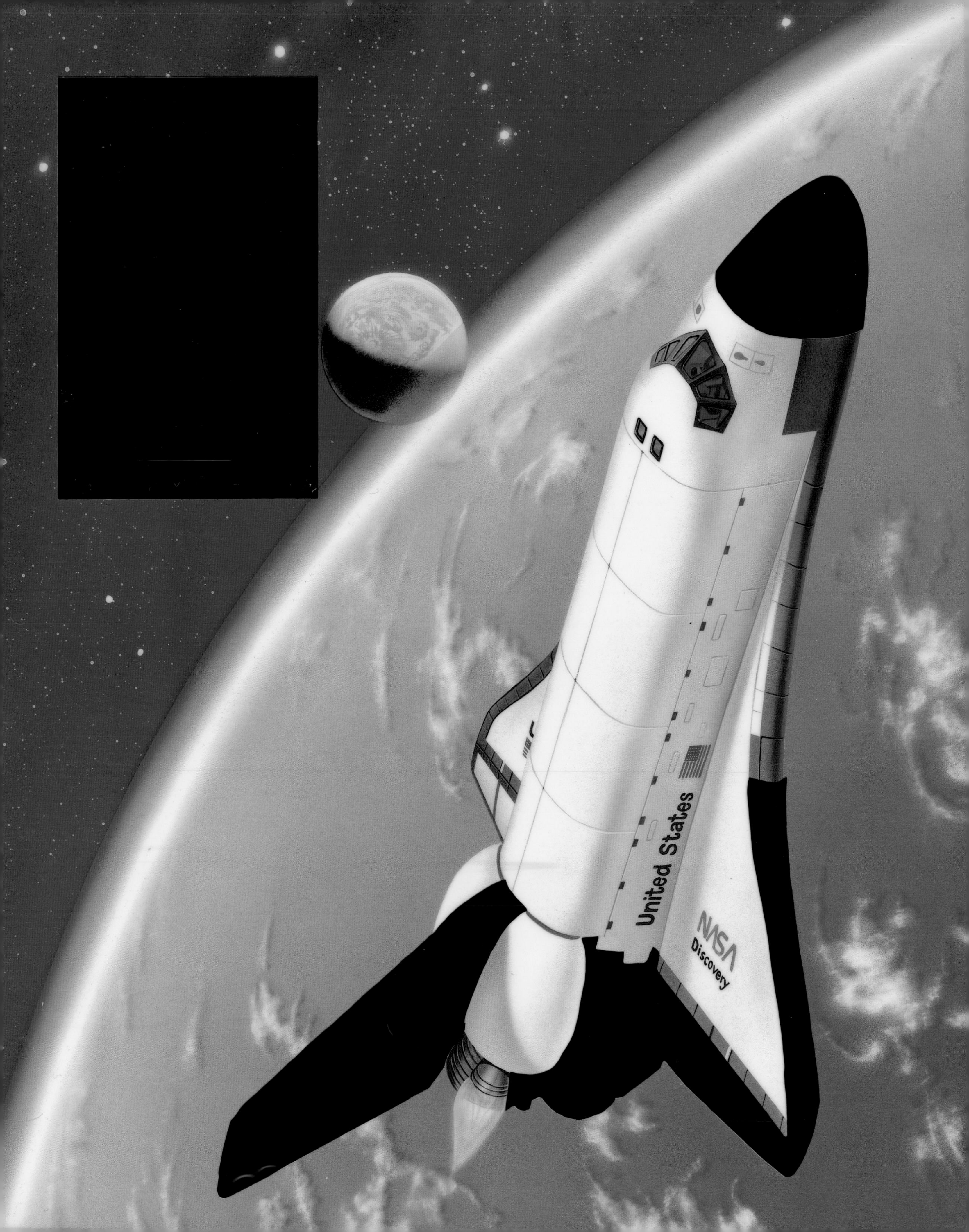
United States
NASA
Discovery

United States
NASA
Discovery

## REPAIRING HUBBLE

**1** Crew compartment
**2** Flight controls
**3** Aft flightdeck (with RMS controls)
**4** Remote Manipulator System (RMS)
**5** Liquid hydrogen and liquid oxygen fuel tanks
**6** Payload bay doors
**7** Support pallet for Hubble
**8** Hubble Space Telescope
**9** Wing ribs and tubular struts
**10** Tanks for manoeuvring engine
**11** Main engine

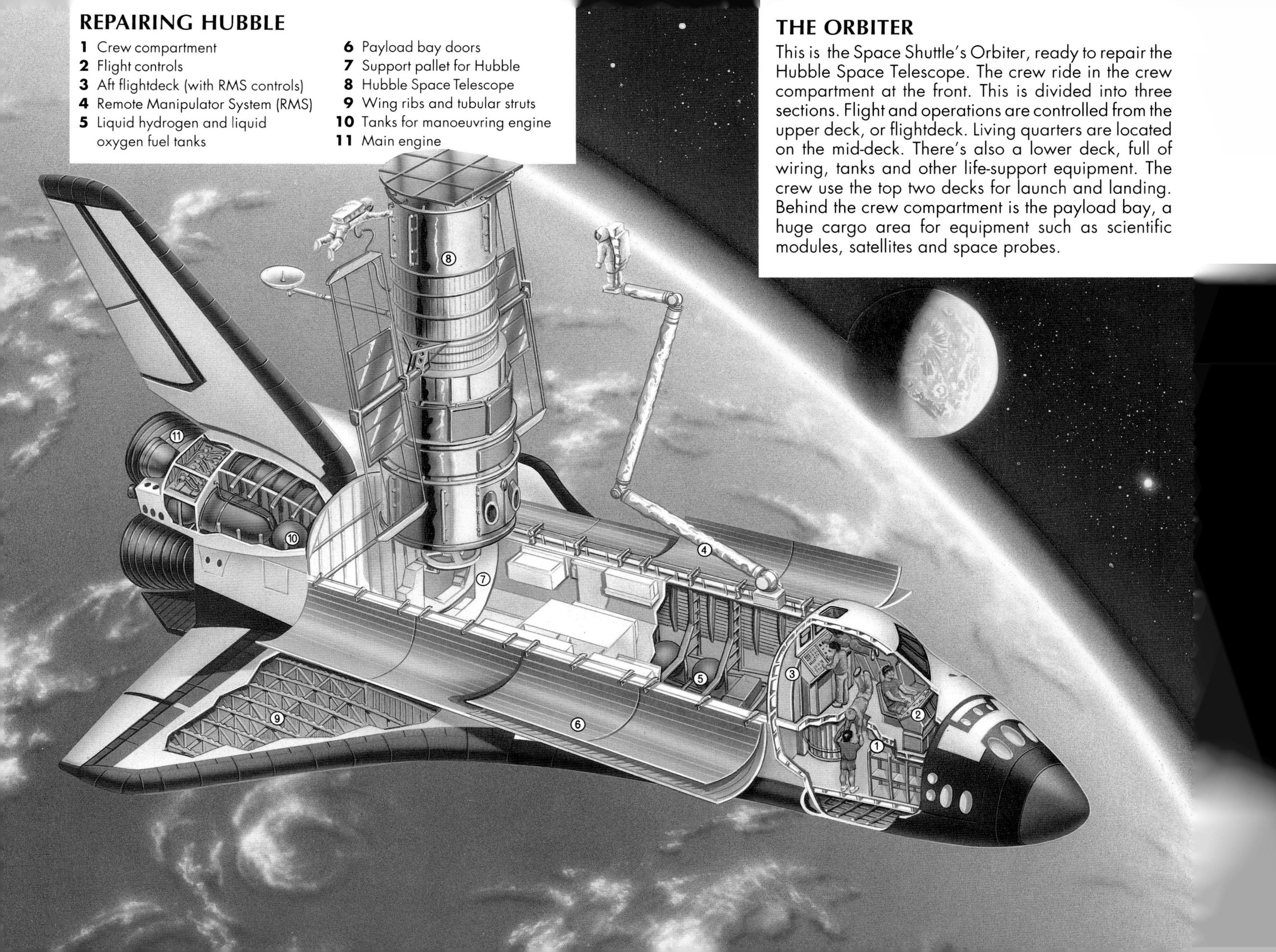

1
2
3
4
5
6
7
8
9
10
11


## THE ORBITER

This is the Space Shuttle's Orbiter, ready to repair the Hubble Space Telescope. The crew ride in the crew compartment at the front. This is divided into three sections. Flight and operations are controlled from the upper deck, or flightdeck. Living quarters are located on the mid-deck. There's also a lower deck, full of wiring, tanks and other life-support equipment. The crew use the top two decks for launch and landing. Behind the crew compartment is the payload bay, a huge cargo area for equipment such as scientific modules, satellites and space probes.

# ORBITAL OPERATIONS

**As soon as the Shuttle is in orbit, the launch phase is completed. The payload bay doors are opened, and orbital operations commence. These include the deployment and retrieval of satellites and space probes.**

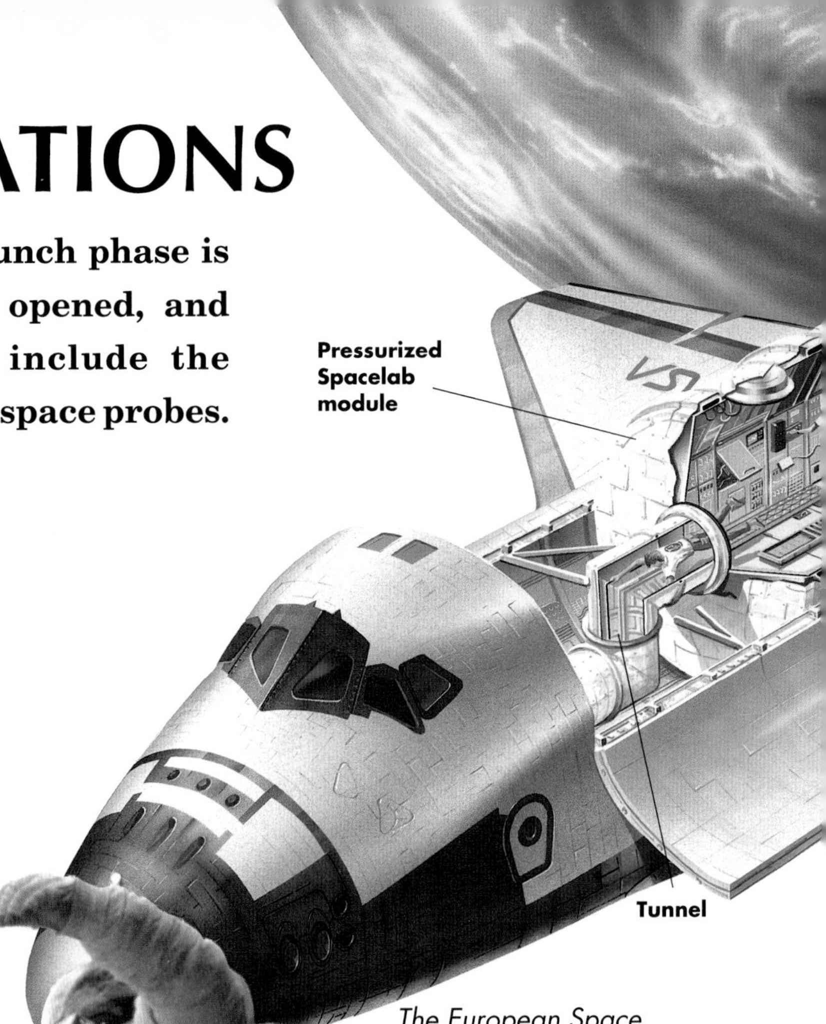

Pressurized Spacelab module
Tunnel


## SATELLITE LAUNCHES

The Shuttle was designed as a commercial and military satellite launch system. Of the hundreds of satellites now orbiting the Earth, over 25 have been launched by the Shuttle. Since 1984, astronauts have retrieved several satellites for repair or return to Earth. This really proved the advantage of the manned Shuttle over unmanned rocket launches. Without the astronauts, such repairs would not have been possible, and millions of pounds worth of satellites would have been lost.

*The European Space Agency has developed the Spacelab scientific research module, which fits in the Orbiter's payload bay.*

## PAYLOADS

The Shuttle is now being used more as a base for scientific research and for launching space probes (see page 36). Probes and satellites are deployed from the bay using spring release mechanisms or, sometimes, a special robot arm, the Remote Manipulator System, or RMS. The Orbiter then moves away from the probe, which then is fired on its way by a rocket called an Inertial Upper Stage (IUS) booster.

Scientific missions are carried out using the Spacelab module, which fits into the Orbiter's payload bay. The Orbiter can carry seven crew for up to 18 days in orbit.

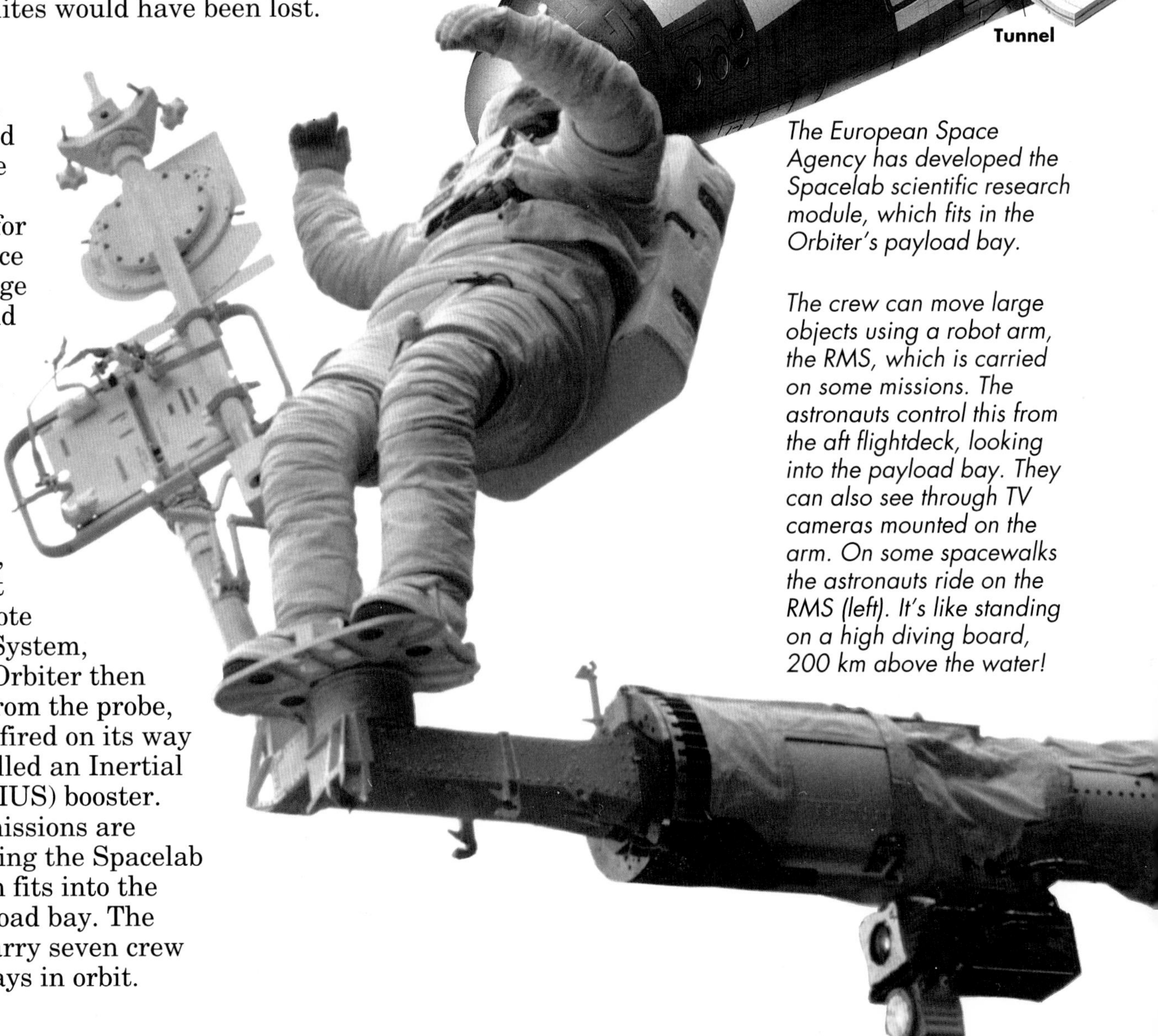

*The crew can move large objects using a robot arm, the RMS, which is carried on some missions. The astronauts control this from the aft flightdeck, looking into the payload bay. They can also see through TV cameras mounted on the arm. On some spacewalks the astronauts ride on the RMS (left). It's like standing on a high diving board, 200 km above the water!*

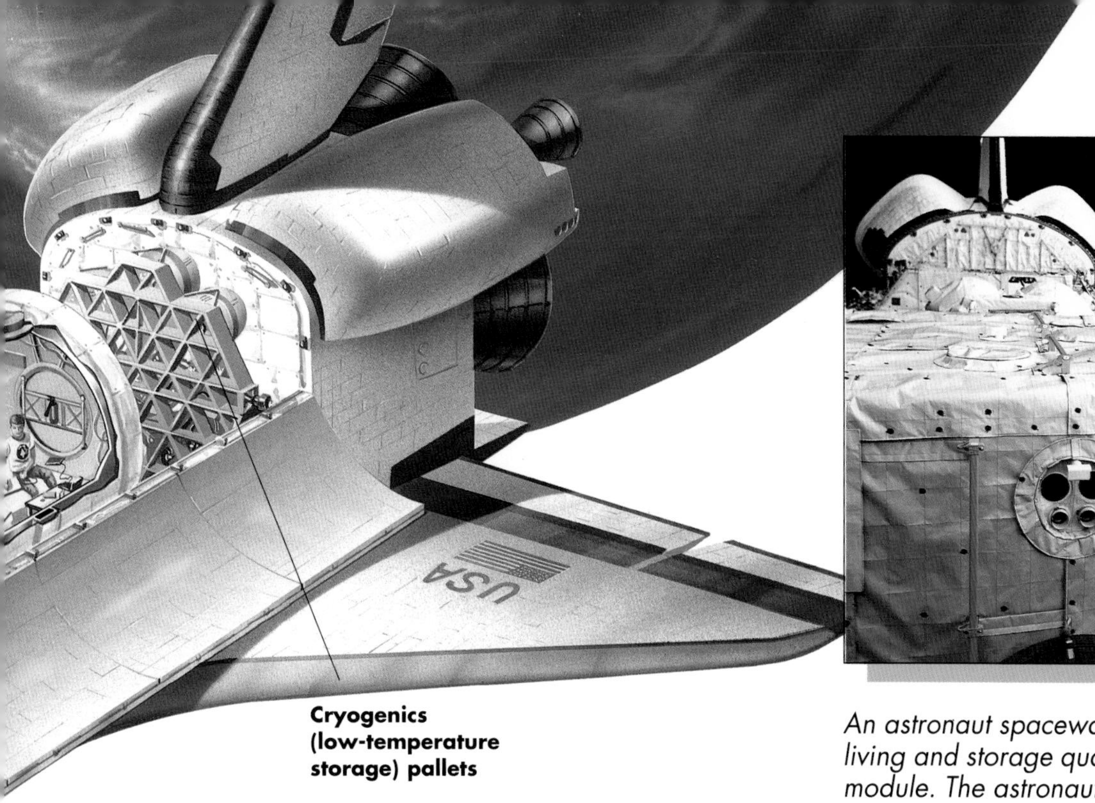
USA
Cryogenics
(low-temperature
storage) pallets

SPACEHAB

*An astronaut spacewalks as the crew make use of the extra living and storage quarters provided by a Spacehab module. The astronaut is riding on the RMS.*

## SPACEWALKS

Sometimes spacewalks are made from the Orbiter, in order to work in the payload bay or retrieve and repair satellites and orbiting scientific equipment, such as the Hubble Space Telescope (see page 34). During the repair of a communications satellite in 1991, the astronauts were in their spacesuits for over eight hours! They could only take a few drinks from their drink dispenser, and had to go to the toilet using the suit's in-built toilet system.

*An early Shuttle mission deploys a commercial satellite (right). Astronauts control the deployment from the aft flightdeck, looking through windows. When the payload is released, the astronauts hear a 'clank'!*

Canada

# LIFE IN SPACE

**Joe Allen knows what it is like to fly in space. He made his first spaceflight in 1982 as a mission specialist on the Space Shuttle. Then, in 1985, he made a spacewalk to 'capture' a faulty satellite for repair on Earth.**

*All space explorers must exercise if they are to return to Earth in good condition. Treadmills, exercise bikes and rowing machines have all been used by astronauts. This 'bicycle' used on a recent Shuttle misssion was cushioned on springs so that its vibrations didn't disturb sensitive scientific experiments.*

*The world spins by - Antarctica and Africa, as seen from* Apollo *17 in 1972.*

## IN SPACE

'Just imagine floating in your own spaceship! Peering out, you watch the oceans and islands and green hills of Earth passing by your windows at break-neck speed. I nearly wrote "*below* your windows", but in the weightless world of space your sense of "up" is completely gone. There is no "above" and no "below" in orbital flight. You just float by the window and look at the scene moving past at five miles per second. Are *you* speeding by the continents and oceans, or are you just hovering in a magical gondola and watching the *world* turn beside you?'

## AT WORK

As the spacecraft orbits the Earth, astronauts do not have a normal day and night as we do. Therefore ship time for the crew is set to the time in Mission Control on Earth.

In orbit, the astronauts are working in zero-gravity. This makes it difficult to keep still when using equipment, so foot loops are provided. Outside the spacecraft, there are tethers and foot restraints for spacewalking astronauts, so they don't drift off into space. In fact, spacecraft designers now ask astronauts to help design work benches, tools and controls, to make their working day more comfortable and productive.

In space, it is very easy to forget that objects float away if not held down. If astronauts lose something, they look for it near the air filters, where the air conditioning might have sucked it. One astronaut's watch was found four missions later!

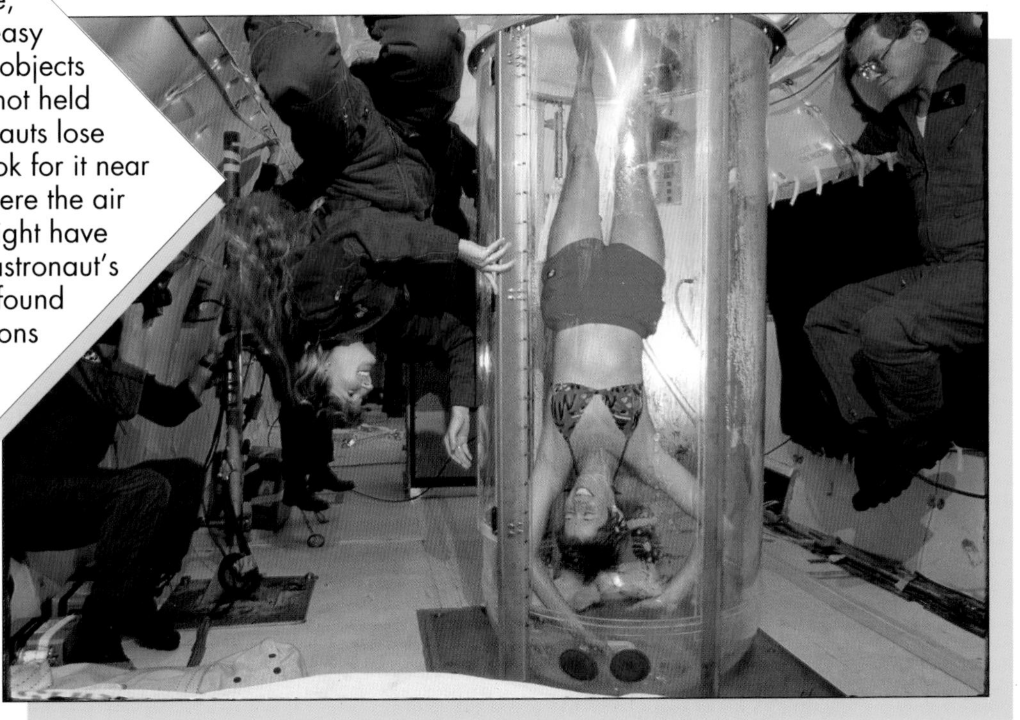

*Astronauts wash using wet and dry towels. Here the 'Vomit Comet' aircraft (see page 9) is being used to test a new 'whole-body zero-g' shower for a future space station.*

*Sleep stations or sleeping bags are provided for the crew (right). Scientific missions are usually completed by two shifts of astronauts, which allows two weeks work on a one-week mission. This means that some astronauts are trying to sleep while others are working.*

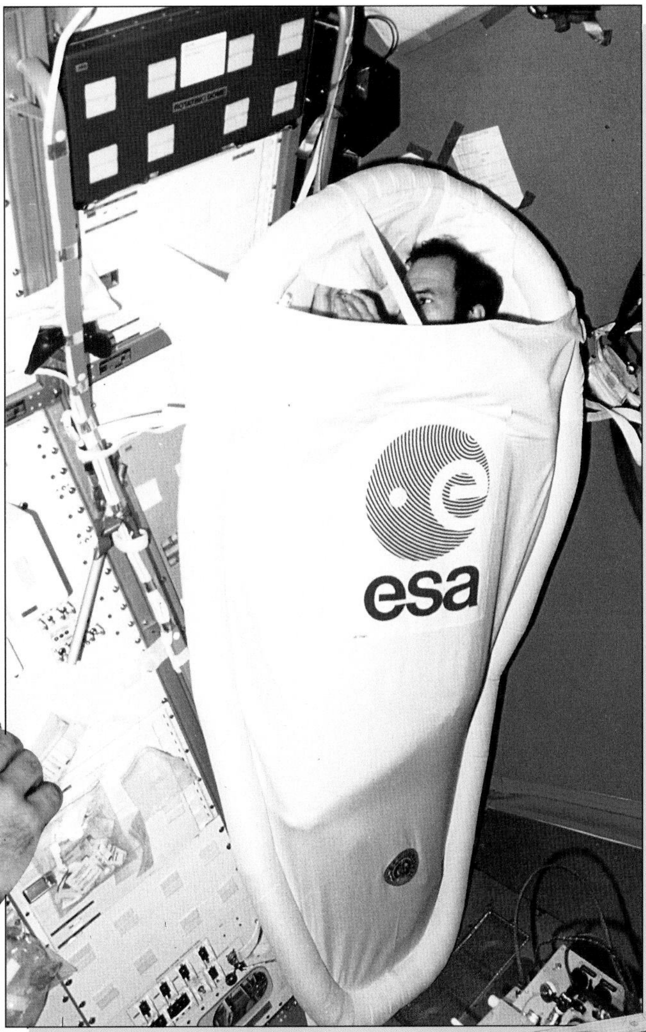
esa

*This is a typical food selection for astronauts (below). They also eat real fruit and M&M's. On Earth, our stomachs expand as we eat food. In space, zero gravity means the astonauts' stomachs 'float', and feel full all the time. However, most astronauts don't lose their appetite, so they still eat a healthy diet!*

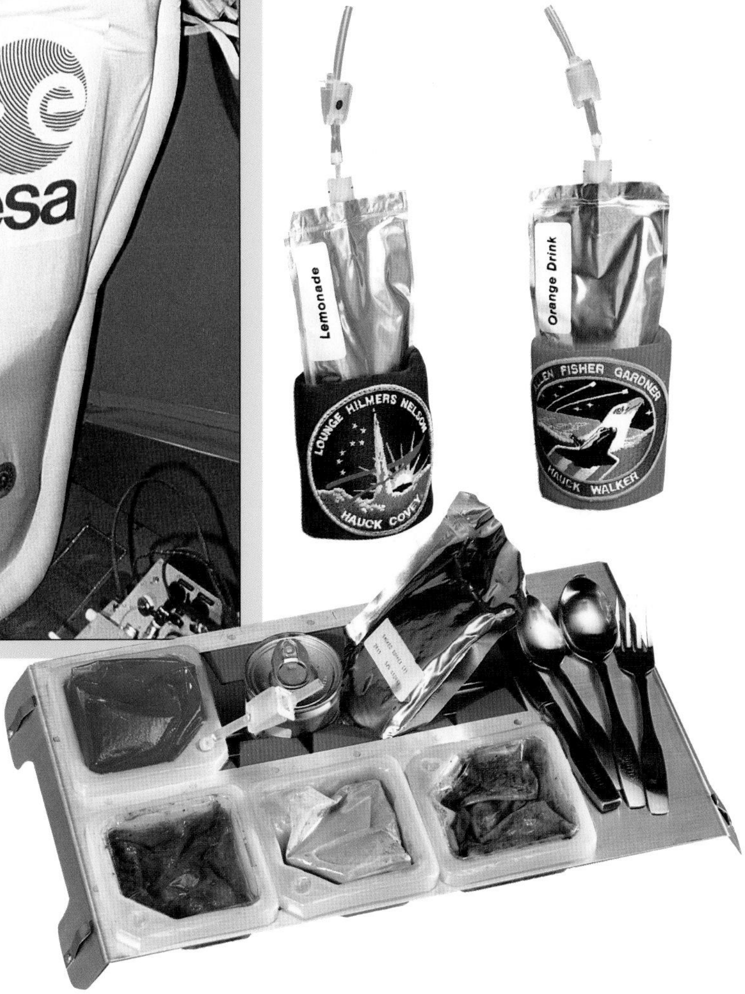
Lemonade
Orange Drink
LOUNGE HILMERS NELSON
HAUCK COVEY
FISHER GARDNER
HAUCK WALKER

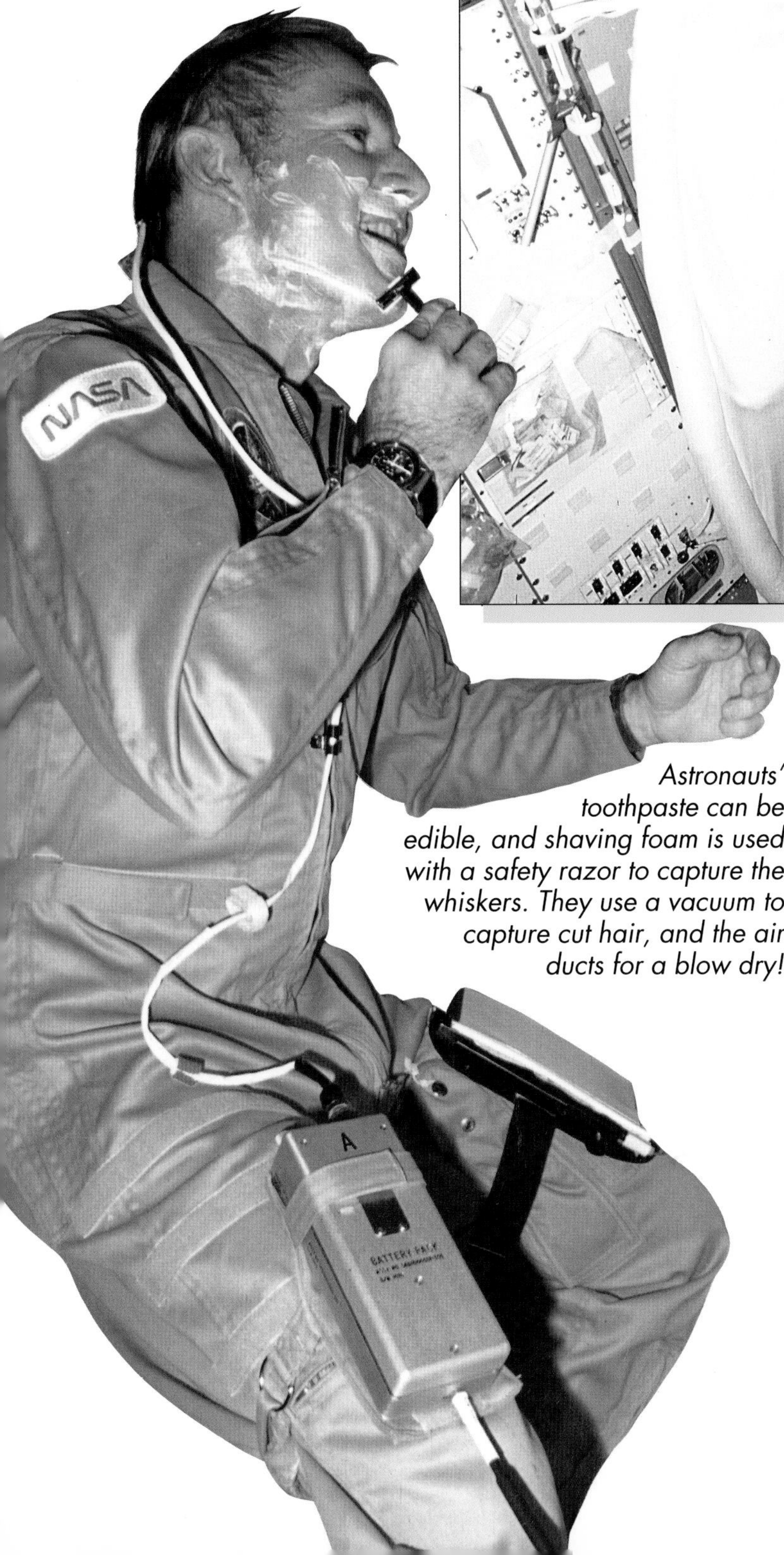
NASA
A

*Astronauts' toothpaste can be edible, and shaving foam is used with a safety razor to capture the whiskers. They use a vacuum to capture cut hair, and the air ducts for a blow dry!*

## WASTE DISPOSAL

Of course, astronauts need to go to the toilet. A spacecraft's toilet is usually worked by a vacuum system that sucks waste down into a reservoir. If the vacuum pump is too strong, the astronaut gets stuck to the seat. This is better than having too *weak* a seal, which lets waste seep out and float in mid-air! It is also an improvement on the *Apollo* missions, when the astronauts had to go into a bag. This was sealed to the body with a strong sticky tape that also pulled the hair from the astronaut's body! Spacewalking astronauts, who might be in their spacesuit for several hours, have a device like a nappy.

# MADE IN SPACE

**We have gone into space because the universe is there, awaiting exploration and discovery. But have we benefited from the space programme, despite the great cost? Going into space has broadened our understanding of life on Earth, and of the Universe where we live. And everyone on Earth has benefited from spin-offs from the space programme.**

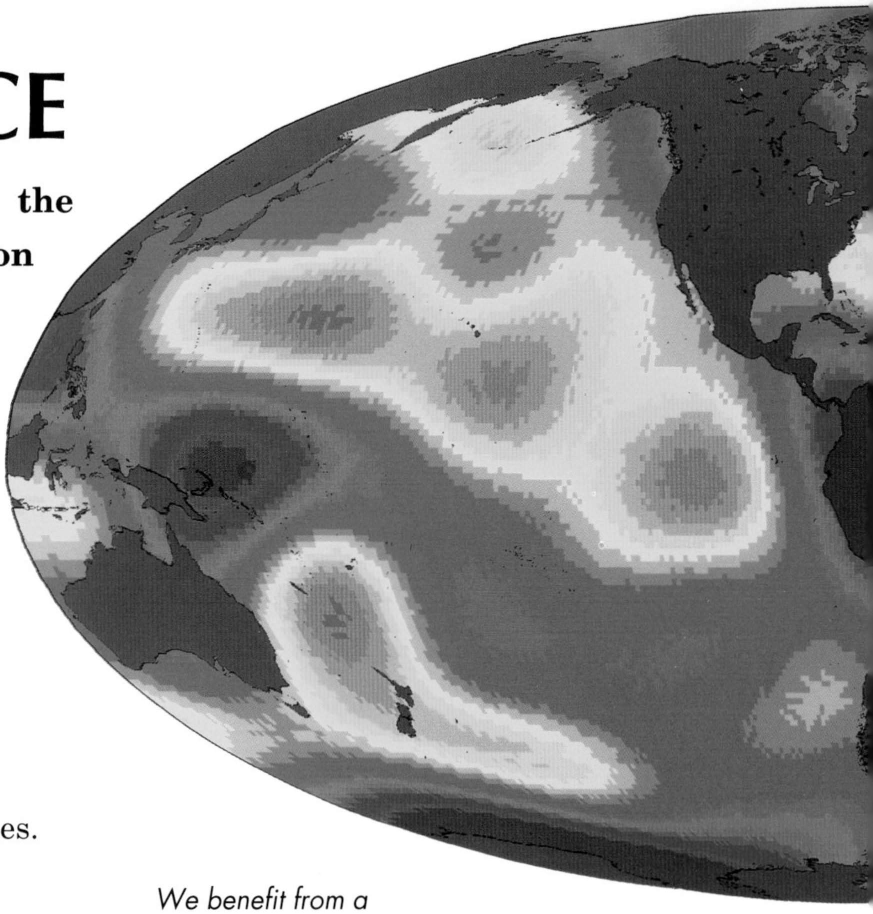

We benefit from a network of satellites in Earth orbit. This false-colour satellite photo gives information about changes in sea levels. Satellites also enable us to see the latest worldwide news events as they happen, and to monitor crop disease, the weather and environmental damage.

## MICROCHIPS

Only now, many years after *Sputnik 1* was launched, is space research in everyone's homes. Today we take for granted the microchip technology in everything from watches to personal computers. Yet this was developed because engineers wanted to put lots of instruments and machines into the spacecraft. Existing computers were far too big to fit into the small spacecraft, and much too heavy for the rockets to lift into orbit. So miniaturization and microchip computers had to be developed.

*The unmanned Long Duration Exposure Facility (LDEF) carried many experiments in Earth orbit. It was supposed to be retrieved in 1985, a year after its deployment. In fact, the Shuttle recaptured it in 1990!*

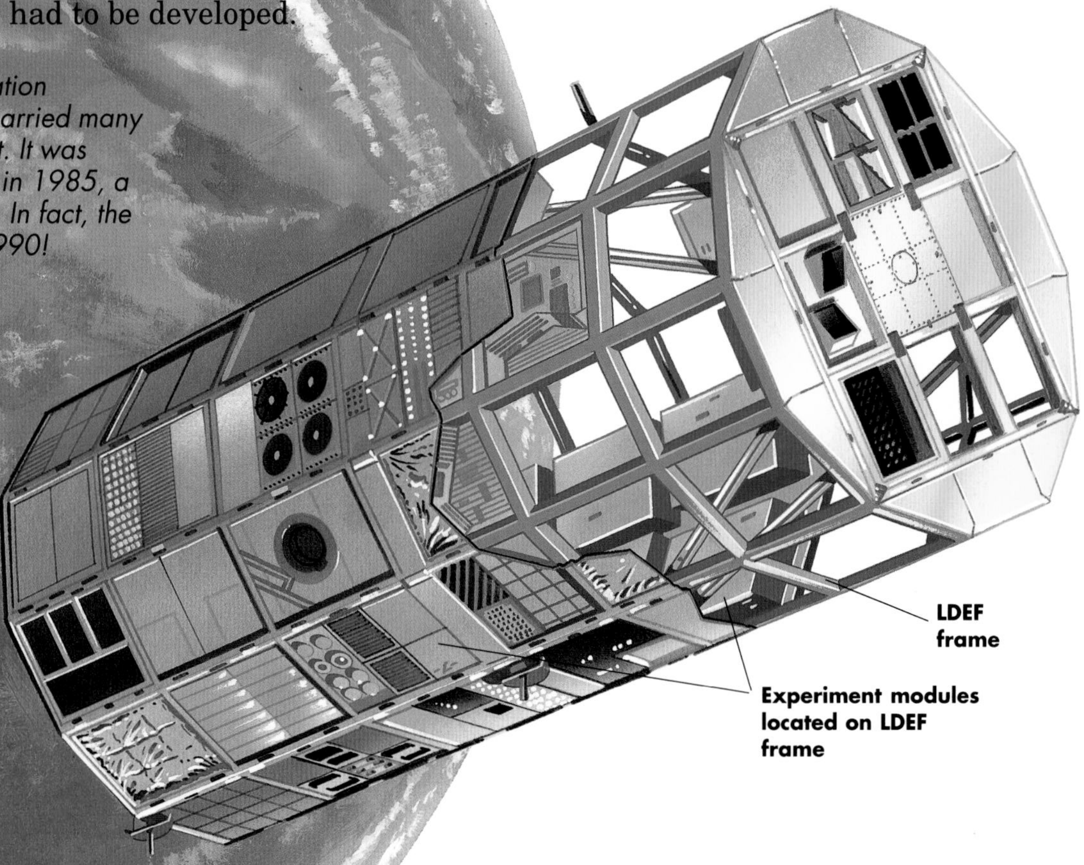
LDEF frame
Experiment modules located on LDEF frame

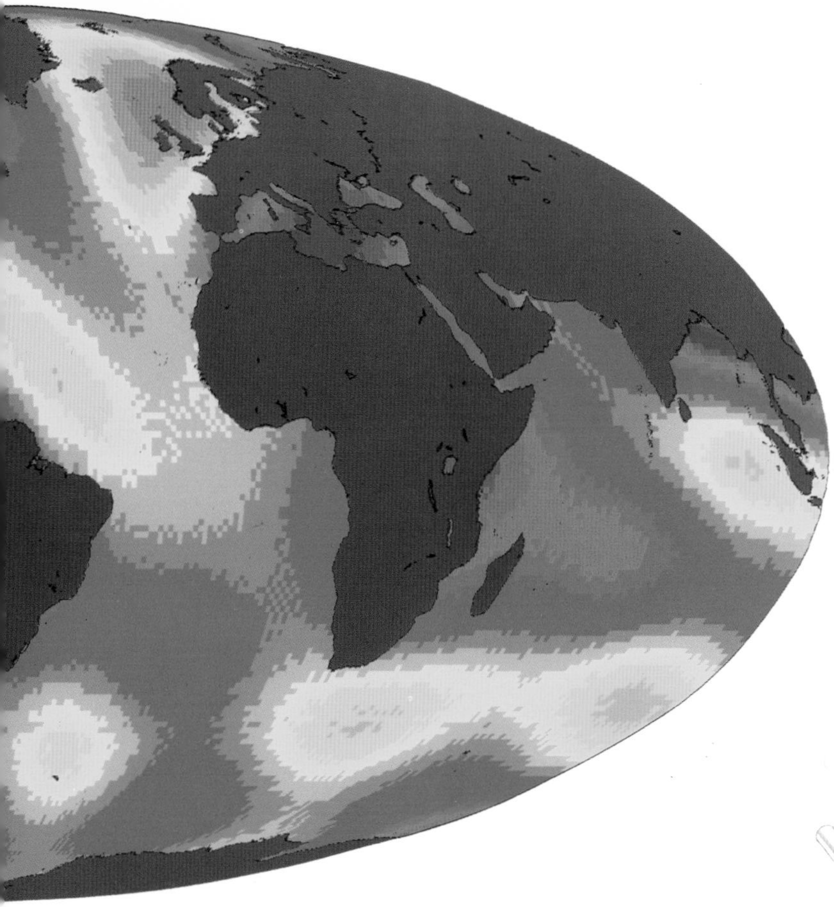

*These space tomatoes were grown from seeds flown in the LDEF. They were part of an experiment to grow food from seeds exposed to spaceflight conditions.*

## MEDICAL DEVELOPMENTS

Some dramatic advances in space research have found their way into medical treatments on Earth. Micro, plastic and keyhole surgery have benefited from the space programme. And surgeons now use a form of spacesuit for protection and medical cleanliness.

Experiments have produced medicines in space. Because of the lack of gravity, these medicines will be purer than ones made on Earth. Surgery in orbit is still some way off, though. There are still many problems to be solved, not least in getting the patient safely to and from orbit!

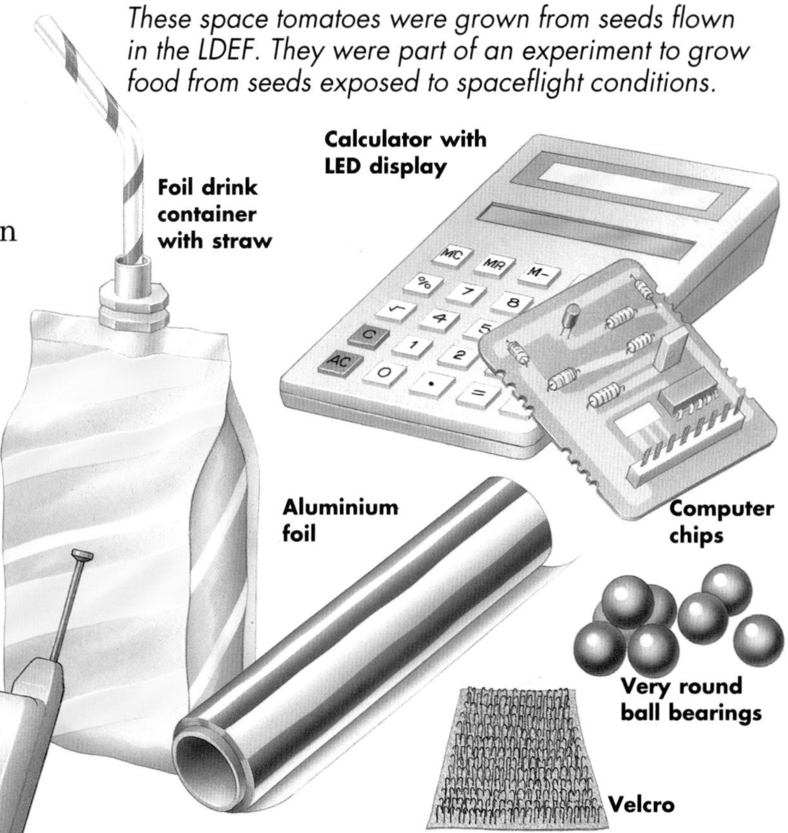
Foil drink container with straw
Calculator with LED display
Aluminium foil
Computer chips
Very round ball bearings
Velcro

*Space technology has found its way into homes on Earth - including methods of preserving and storing food, such as airproof cola cans!*

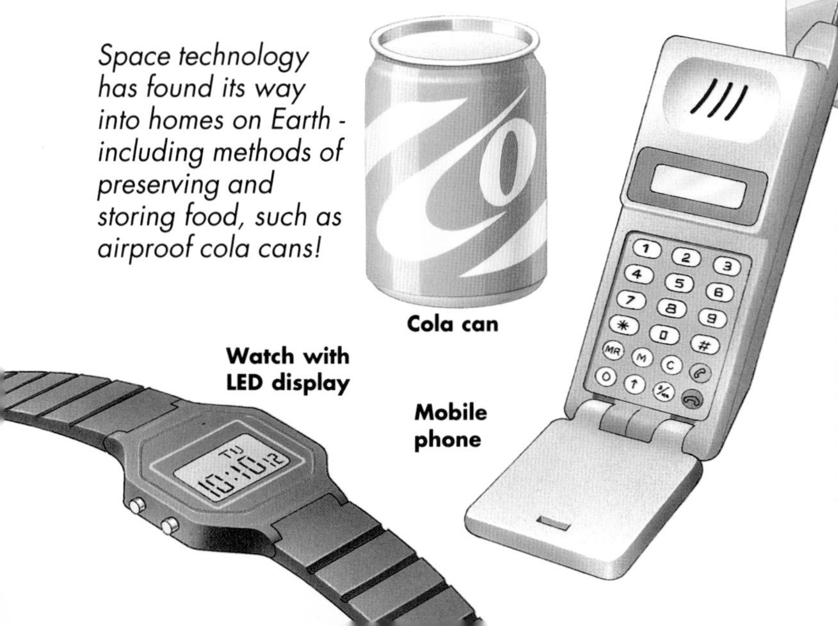
Cola can
Watch with LED display
Mobile phone

## SPACE PRODUCTION

Production of crystals and microchips in space is another new technology. For example, a simple ball bearing made on Earth is still affected by gravity so is not perfectly spherical. In space, there's no gravity, so a truly perfect sphere is formed. Therefore the ball bearing will work more smoothly, and it and the machine it is in will last longer.

# SPACESUITS

**The Extra-Vehicular Activity (EVA) spacesuit is a mini spacecraft. It provides the oxygen, heating, cooling, communication, refreshment and toilet facilities an astronaut needs to work outside the spacecraft. Astronaut Joe Allen describes how he 'suited up' in the Space Shuttle:**

*A crew walks out to the Shuttle. Their bulging pockets are full of items such as gloves, mission data files, sandwiches (in case there's a delay in launching), sunglasses and pens. The basic Shuttle coverall suit and helmet (which has already been placed in the Shuttle) will protect the crew if cabin oxygen is lost during lift-off.*

## BUNDLED UP

'Putting on the EVA spacesuit always reminded me of the feeling I had when my mother dressed me in a very heavy snowsuit. In this case, your shipmates bundle you up. They stuff you in the spacesuit, often with a pat on the back and a butter cookie in the mouth for good luck. Then they put the helmet over your head, snap it into place at the neck ring, and from that moment on *you float in the suit*, your toes gently touching the boots, your head occasionally bobbing up against the helmet.

'You are now floating in a space-age cocoon, and because of its protection you can float right out through the hatch. Using the controls of a Manned Maneuvering Unit (MMU), you can even move yourself away from the mother ship. You are then orbiting the Earth as surely as the Moon orbits the Earth, and you are a satellite!'

*EVA suits must be packaged up for storage in the airlock (right).*

*Every spacesuit must be tested before each mission. Below, an EVA suit's pressure and electronics are being checked.*

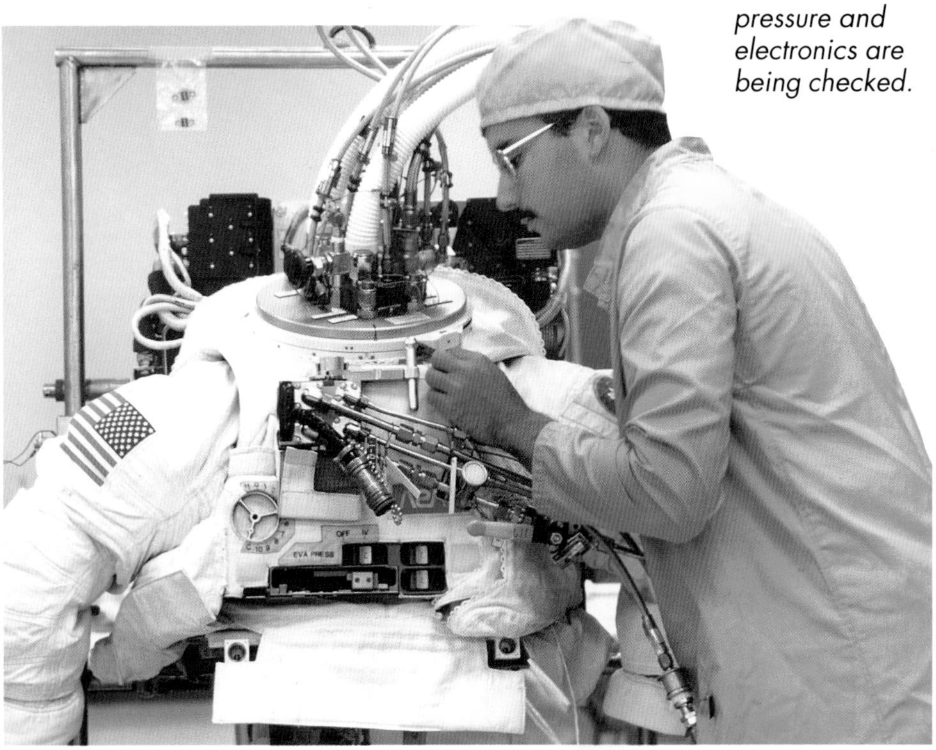

On *Apollo 16*, astronaut Charlie Duke grew taller because of the lack of gravity, and had difficulty getting into his spacesuit. He also got a surprise when his in-suit drink dispenser failed while he was on a moon walk - it gave his hair an orange-juice shampoo!

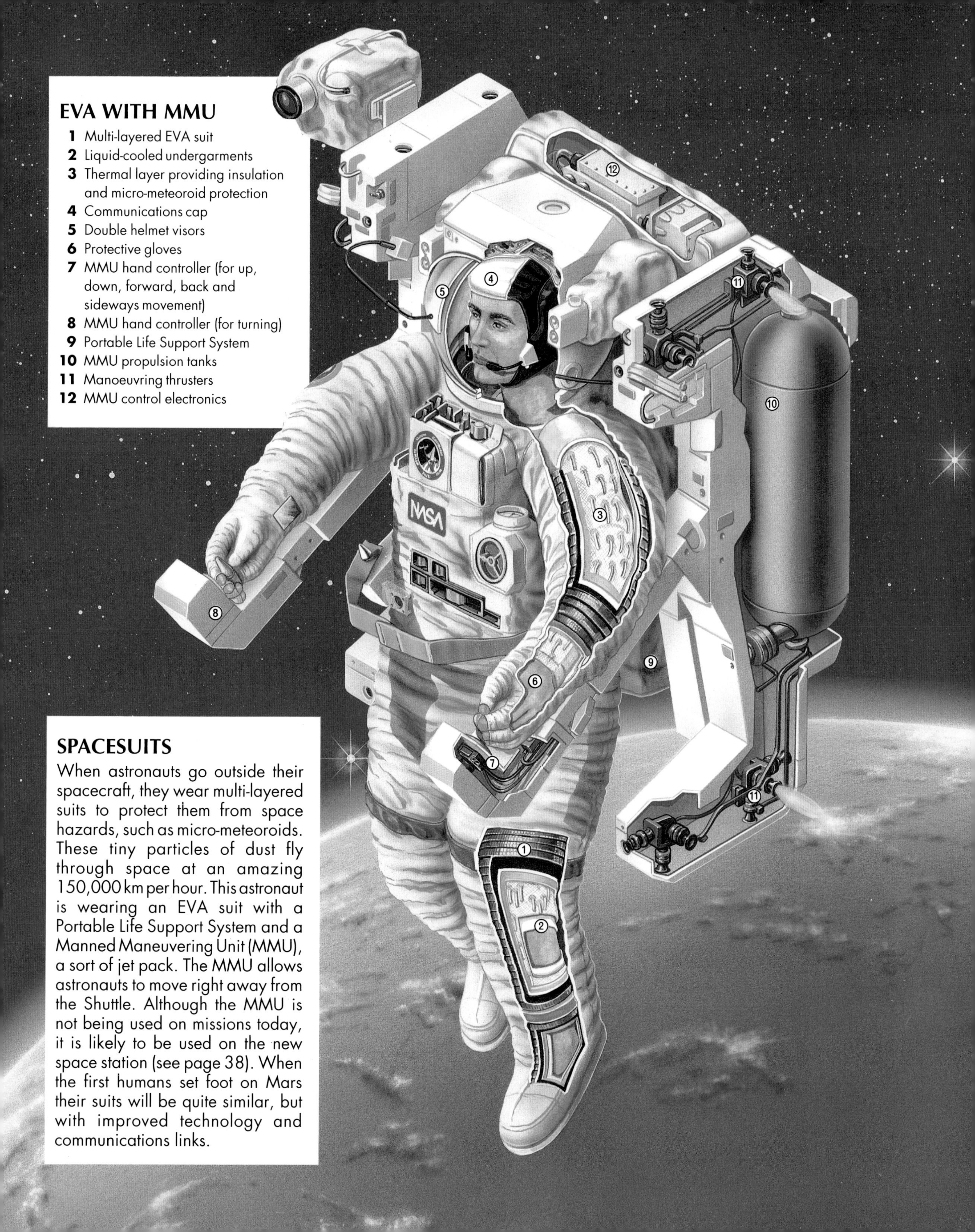

## EVA WITH MMU

**1** Multi-layered EVA suit
**2** Liquid-cooled undergarments
**3** Thermal layer providing insulation and micro-meteoroid protection
**4** Communications cap
**5** Double helmet visors
**6** Protective gloves
**7** MMU hand controller (for up, down, forward, back and sideways movement)
**8** MMU hand controller (for turning)
**9** Portable Life Support System
**10** MMU propulsion tanks
**11** Manoeuvring thrusters
**12** MMU control electronics

## SPACESUITS

When astronauts go outside their spacecraft, they wear multi-layered suits to protect them from space hazards, such as micro-meteoroids. These tiny particles of dust fly through space at an amazing 150,000 km per hour. This astronaut is wearing an EVA suit with a Portable Life Support System and a Manned Maneuvering Unit (MMU), a sort of jet pack. The MMU allows astronauts to move right away from the Shuttle. Although the MMU is not being used on missions today, it is likely to be used on the new space station (see page 38). When the first humans set foot on Mars their suits will be quite similar, but with improved technology and communications links.

# EYE IN THE SKY

**The deployment of the Hubble Space Telescope in 1990 was a huge advance in space exploration. Over 600 kilometres above the Earth, Hubble's view of the Universe would not be distorted by the Earth's atmosphere. It would also be able to 'see' types of radiation that are absorbed by the atmosphere before they reach telescopes on Earth.**

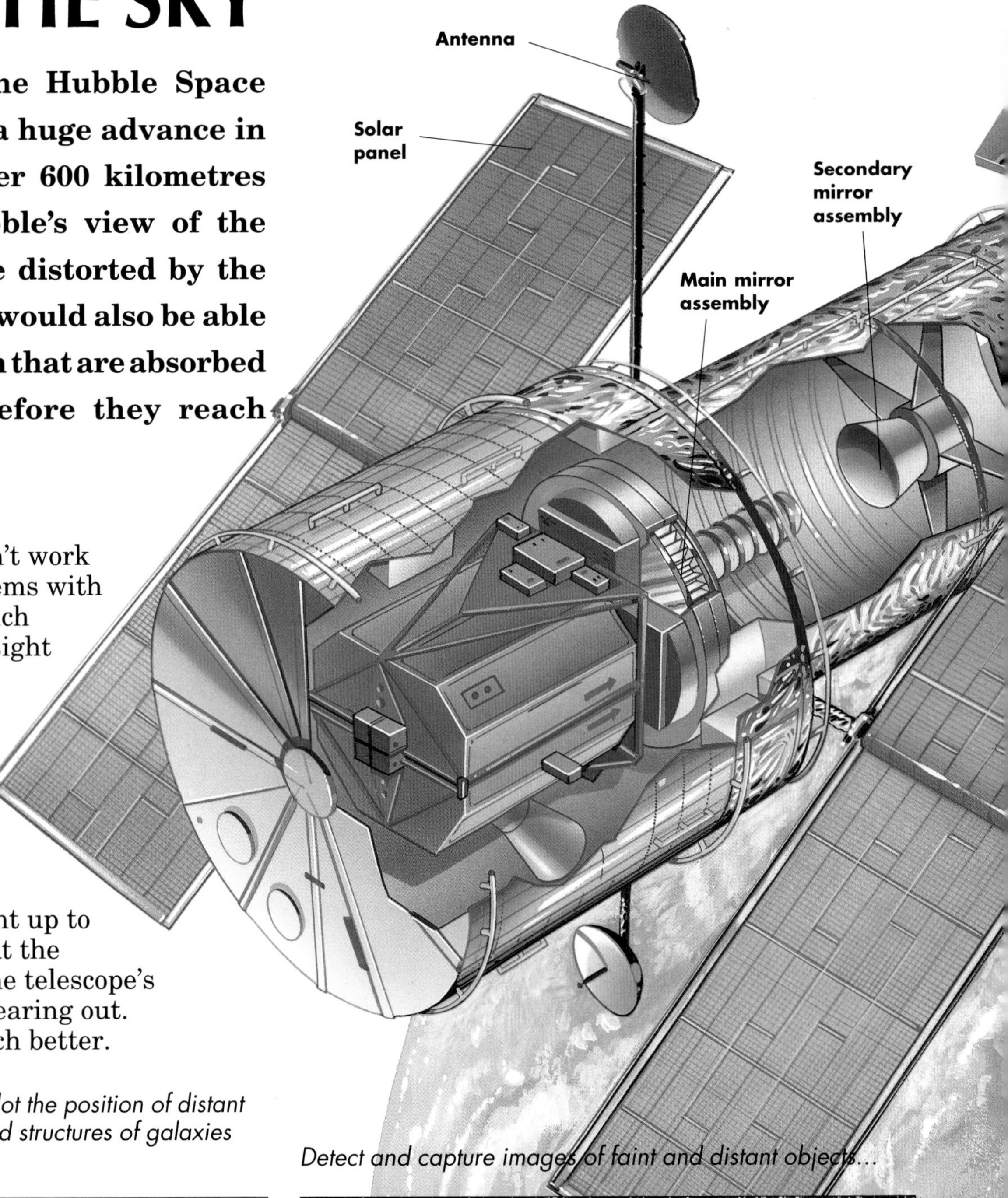
Antenna
Solar panel
Secondary mirror assembly
Main mirror assembly

## HUBBLE TROUBLE

Unfortunately, Hubble didn't work properly. There were problems with its huge mirror system, which meant that the telescope's sight was blurred! Fortunately, using new computer techniques, scientists were still able to detect many more stars in space, and calculate their age and distance much more accurately. Eventually, the Shuttle astronauts were sent up to adjust the mirror system. At the same time, they replaced the telescope's solar panels, which were wearing out. Hubble is now working much better.

*Hubble's many instruments can plot the position of distant galaxies, and observe the detailed structures of galaxies and planets...*

*Detect and capture images of faint and distant objects...*

Aperture door

*The Hubble Space Telescope.*

## ORBITING OBSERVATORIES

Hubble is one of several large observatories in orbit. When it is working properly, Hubble can see objects that are 50 times fainter and seven times farther away than any ground-based telescope. Information from Hubble, plus data from other orbiting 'Great Observatories' such as the Compton Gamma Ray Observatory and the Upper Atmospheric Research Satellite, will teach us more about our Universe. It will also be used to plan future space missions and experiments.

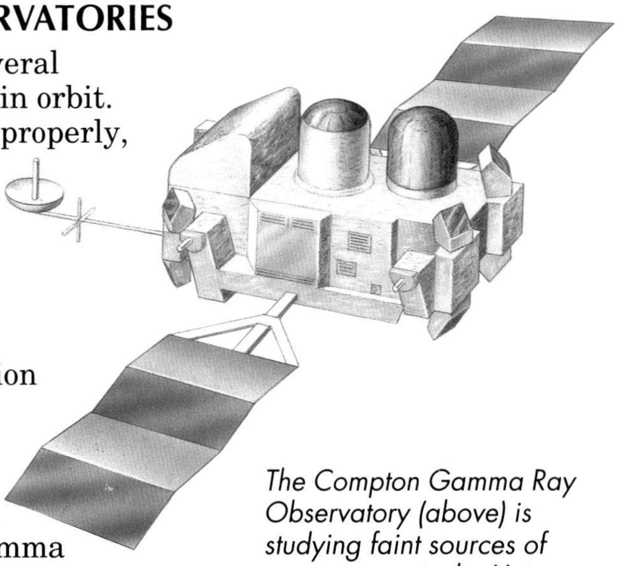

*The Compton Gamma Ray Observatory (above) is studying faint sources of gamma rays in the Universe.*

*The Earth's atmosphere is struck by a wide range of rays and particles (below). Only visible light, infra-red and radio waves actually reach the ground and can be observed by ground telescopes.*

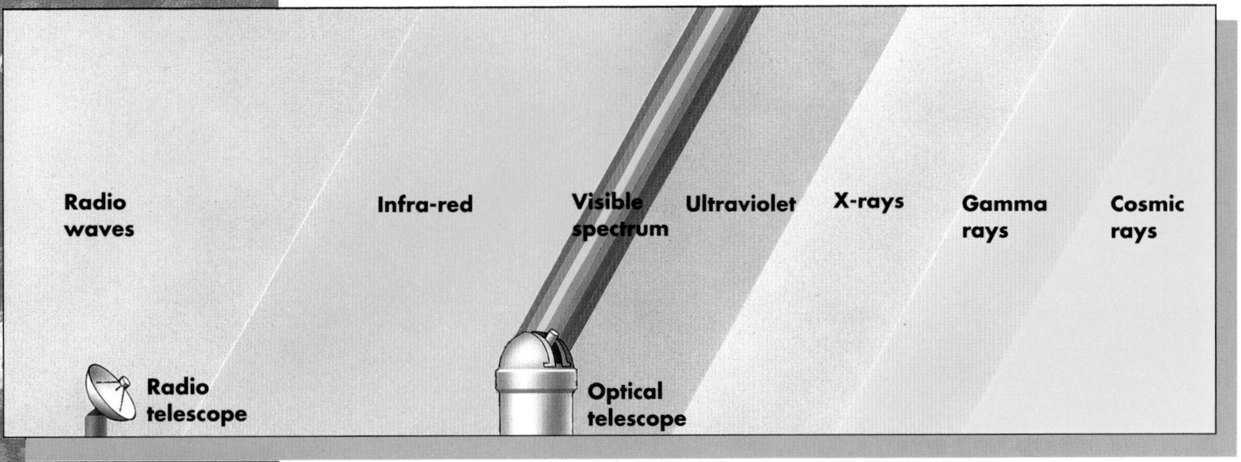
Radio waves
Infra-red
Visible spectrum
Ultraviolet
X-rays
Gamma rays
Cosmic rays
Radio telescope
Optical telescope

*Detect and measure the spectra of faint objects...*

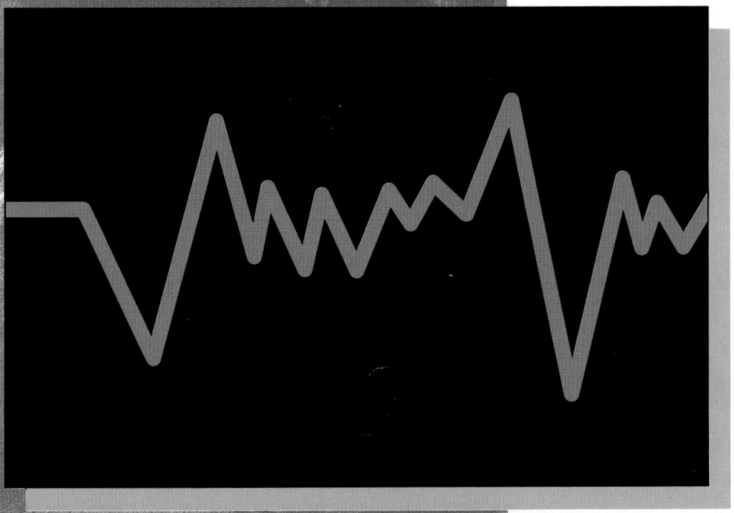

*And track and map the position of stars.*

# SPACE PROBES

**As well as exploring the Moon and conditions in space, we have been sending 'probes' to explore the planets that are much further away. America and Russia have explored Mars, Venus and Mercury, and American probes have also ventured out to explore the giant planets such as Jupiter.**

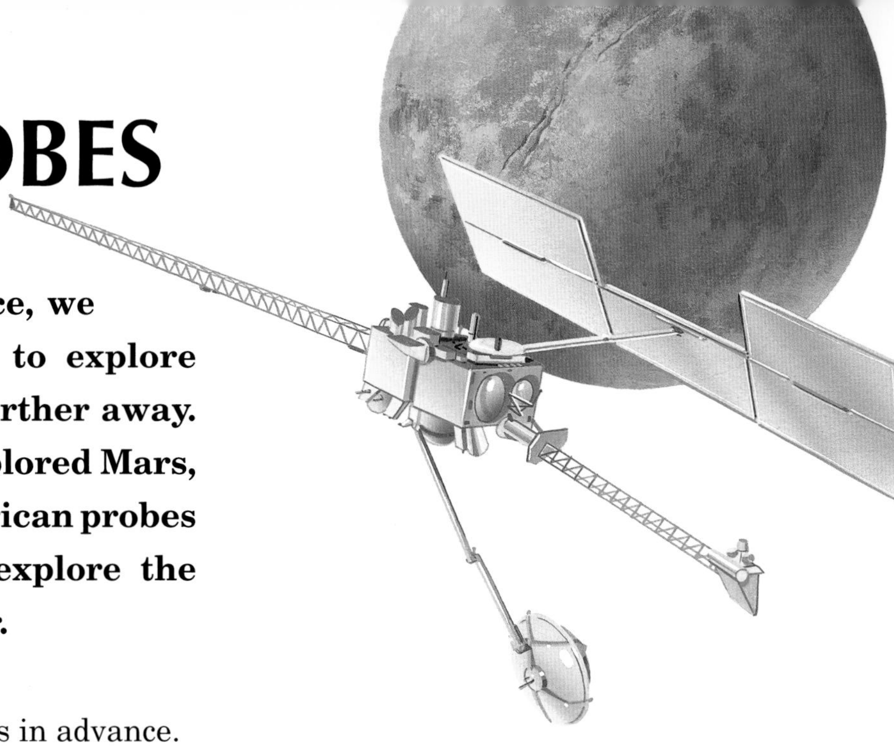

*Not all space probes are successful. In 1993, mission control lost contact with the Mars Observer (above). This meant scientists were unable to gather some data for a planned landing on Mars.*

## PLANNING THE PROBE

Scientists must plan missions years in advance. They must decide exactly what information they will try to gather. If the probe fails, it is very costly in time and money to send another one. It takes several years for a probe to reach one of the outer planets. Also, a probe can only be launched if the planets will be in certain positions, so that the probe can use each planet's gravity to swing it on its way.

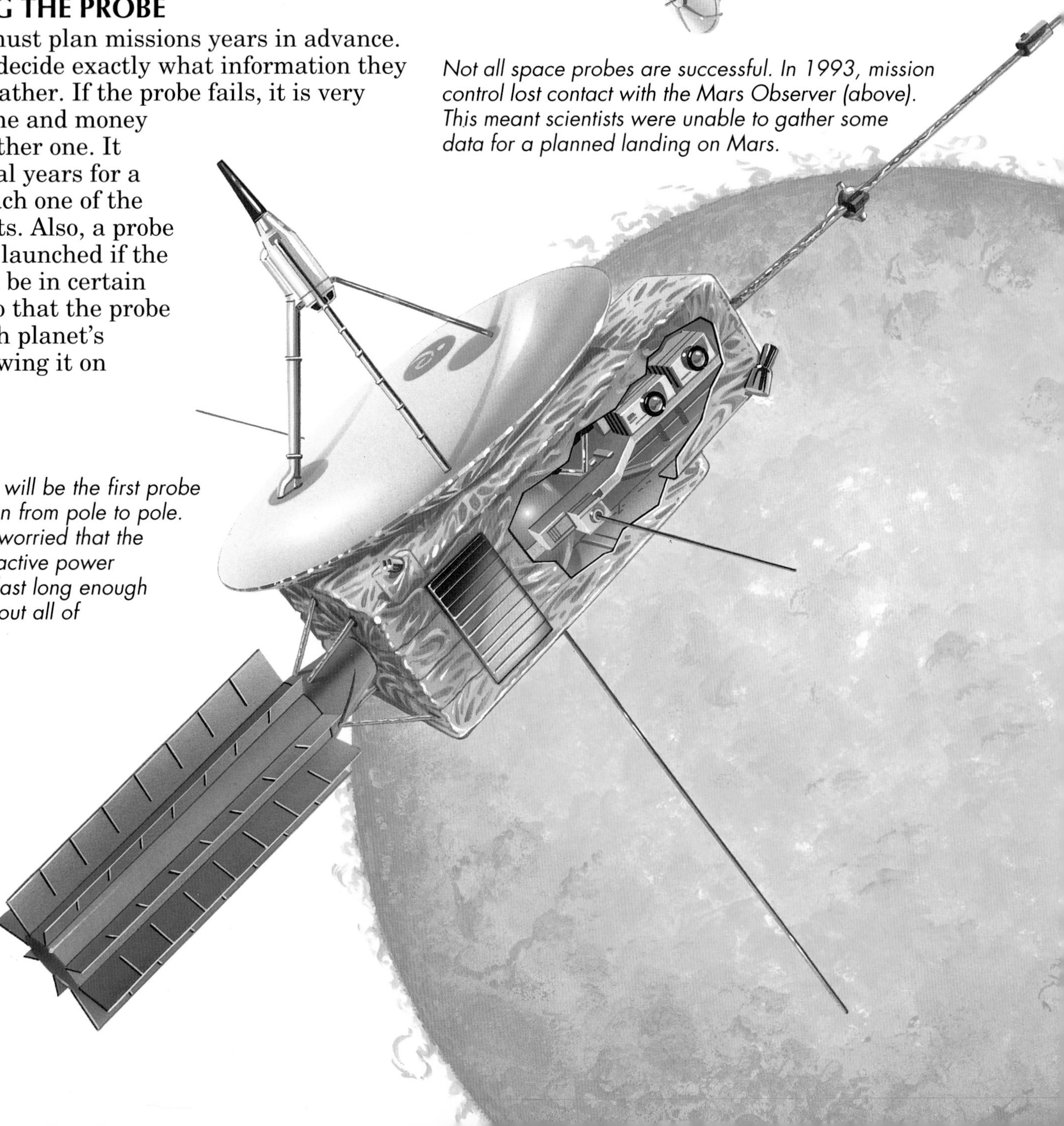

*Ulysses (right) will be the first probe to orbit the Sun from pole to pole. Scientists are worried that the probe's radioactive power pack will not last long enough for it to carry out all of its mission.*

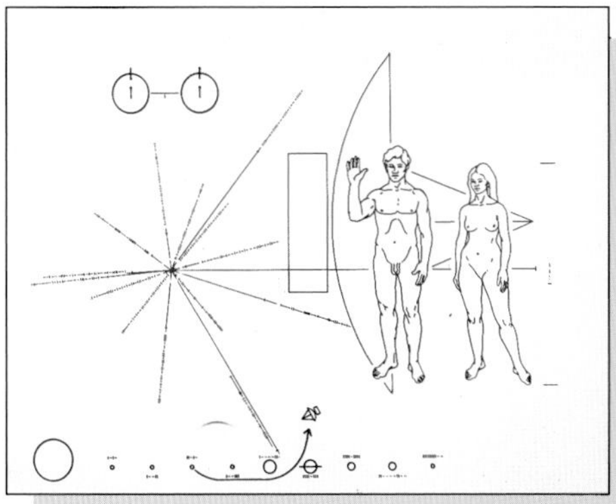

*Having flown by Jupiter,* Pioneer 10 *and* 11 *passed into deep space. In case the probes are found by another advanced civilization, scientists attached this plaque telling the 'aliens' about the Earth and its life.*

## THE GIANT PLANETS

The first deep space probes were *Pioneer 10* and *11* in the 1970s, but it was the two *Voyager* probes that finally gave spectacular views of Jupiter, Saturn, Neptune and Uranus as well as their moons and ring systems. They successfully used the 'sling shot' technique (explained on page 18) to travel to edge of the solar system.

Today, space probes are going to specific planets. *Galileo* (see page 18) will release a probe into Jupiter's atmosphere, and *Magellan's* radar has recently scanned Venus.

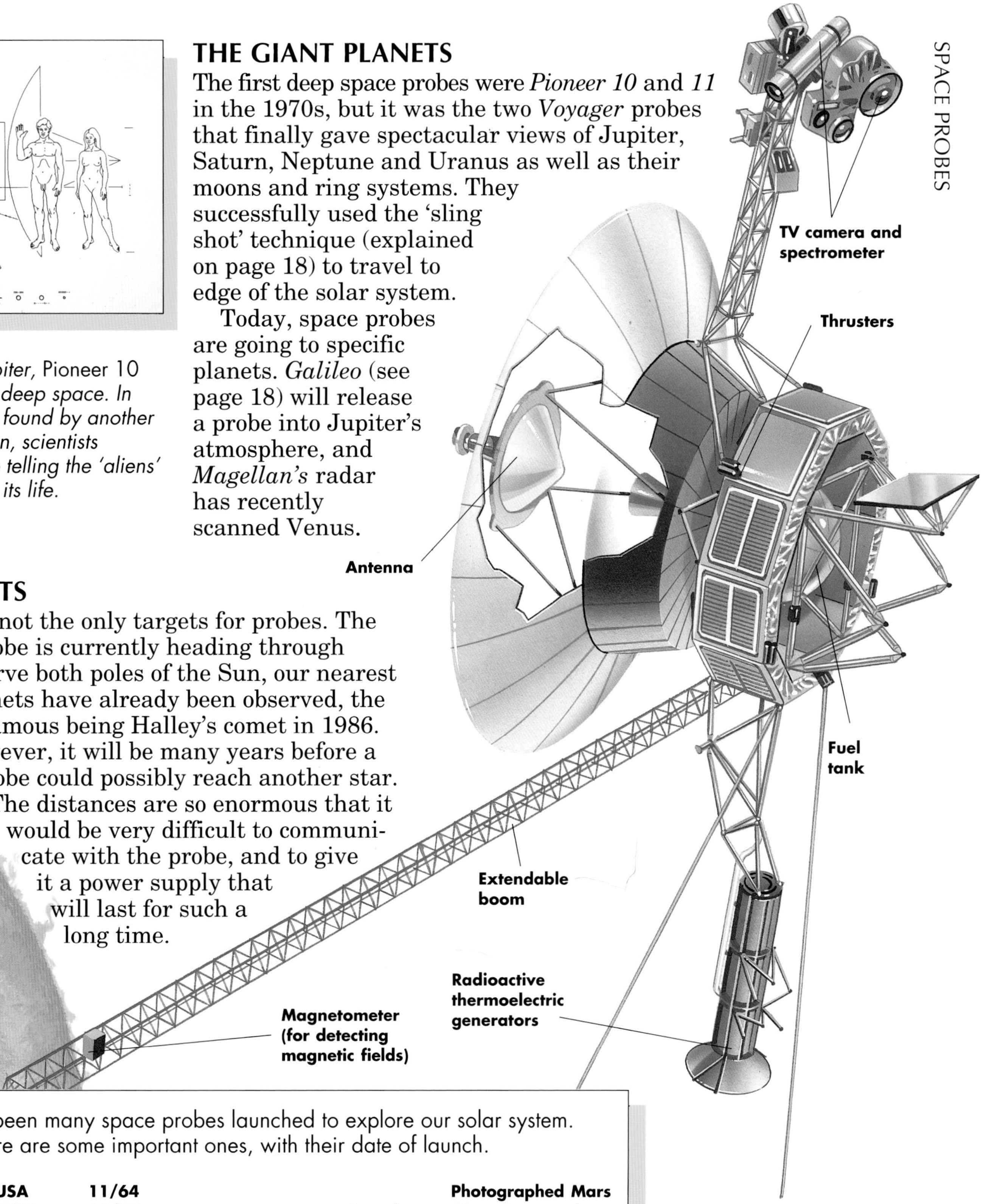

TV camera and spectrometer
Thrusters
Antenna
Fuel tank
Extendable boom
Radioactive thermoelectric generators
Magnetometer (for detecting magnetic fields)


## OTHER TARGETS

The planets are not the only targets for probes. The *Ulysses* solar probe is currently heading through space to observe both poles of the Sun, our nearest star. Comets have already been observed, the most famous being Halley's comet in 1986. However, it will be many years before a probe could possibly reach another star. The distances are so enormous that it would be very difficult to communicate with the probe, and to give it a power supply that will last for such a long time.

There have been many space probes launched to explore our solar system. Here are some important ones, with their date of launch.

| | | | |
|---|---|---|---|
| ***Mariner IV*** | **USA** | **11/64** | **Photographed Mars** |
| ***Venera 4*** | **USSR** | **06/67** | **Sent data on Venus' atmosphere** |
| ***Venera 7*** | **USSR** | **08/70** | **Sent data from Venus' surface** |
| ***Mariner IX*** | **USA** | **05/71** | **First probe to orbit Mars** |
| ***Pioneer 10*** | **USA** | **02/72** | **Flew past Jupiter. Became first spacecraft to pass all outer planets. Now nine thousand million kilometres from the Sun** |
| ***Pioneer-Saturn*** | **USA** | **04/73** | **Flew past Saturn** |
| ***Mariner X*** | **USA** | **11/73** | **First probe to fly by two planets: Venus and Mercury** |
| ***Voyager 2*** | **USA** | **08/77** | **Flew past Jupiter, Saturn, Uranus and Neptune** |
| ***Voyager 1*** | **USA** | **09/77** | **Flew past Jupiter, Saturn** |
| ***Giotto*** | **Europe** | **07/85** | **Flew past Halley's Comet. Discovered centre of comet is an icy ball containing organic compounds** |

*The* Voyager *probes (above) have now left our solar system.* Voyager 1 *is more than eight thousand million kilometres from the Sun - that's nearly 50 times further from the Sun than the Earth is.*

# SPACE STATIONS

**One of the best ways to prepare for exploring space and conducting scientific experiments is from a space station. As with most ideas in spaceflight, the idea of space stations could be found in books long before the first satellite flew.**

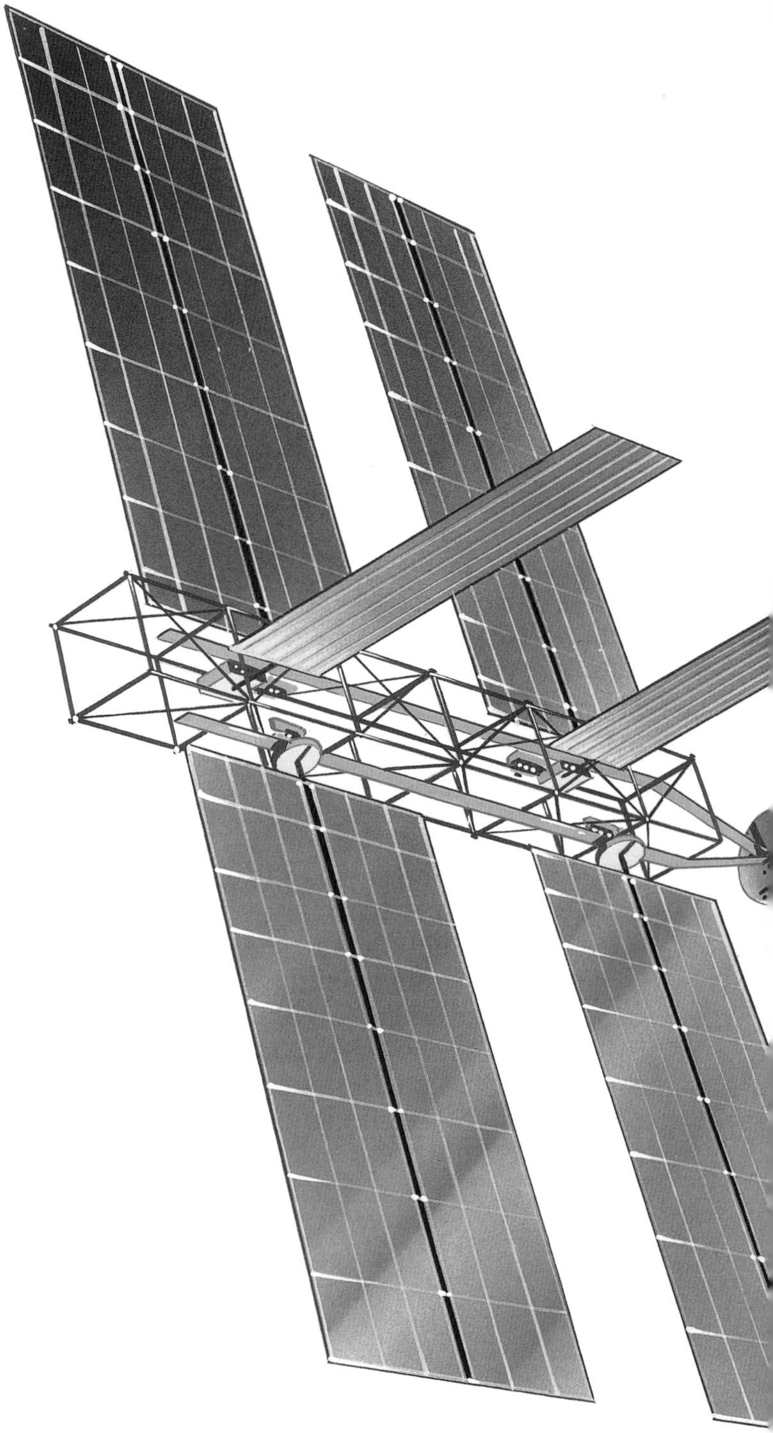

## SCIENCE FICTION - SCIENCE FACT

Science fiction space stations are always huge, complex designs, almost as large as a small city on Earth. When the first space stations flew they were little more than the size of the inside of a house. The American 100-tonne *Skylab* was a converted moon rocket stage, and the Russian *Salyut* had an interior about the size of a London tube train carriage.

These first space stations carried out valuable research, but size and power restricted the work they could do. Bigger stations, that would last for much longer, were needed. Therefore the *Salyut* stations grew to the *Mir* space complex (see page 41), but the largest space station plans are for the American international programme.

*The first US space station, Skylab, is seen orbiting with just one solar wing (below). Its other wing was lost during the launch. Three teams of three astronauts spent 28, 59 and 84 days in this former Saturn V moon rocket stage. Skylab eventually dropped into the Earth's atmosphere. In 1979 it burned up and scattered debris across Australia.*

## A NEW STATION

The design and name of the station has changed over the years, as the cost of the programme has increased. The basic station consists of a group of modules linked together and powered by solar panels. Countries and space agencies from around the world will provide a pressurized module or major elements of the station.

This large complex is expected to remain in orbit for up to 30 years. It will probably be commanded by a scientist. Its crew will include people from many nations, in a research programme similar to that conducted on bases in the Earth's Antarctic polar region.

## RESEARCH AND EXPERIMENTS

The space station's research will concentrate on life sciences and medical experiments. For example, studying the effects of weightlessness on the body is of importance for long spaceflights to planets such as Mars. Research into materials will be continued, and observations of the Earth will be another important part of the station's work. The station will eventually be a base for manned exploration of the Moon and Mars.

*The inside of the international space station will probably resemble this 1992 view inside Spacelab-J (left). Astronaut Mae Jemison floats in zero gravity, surrounded by instruments and storage units.*

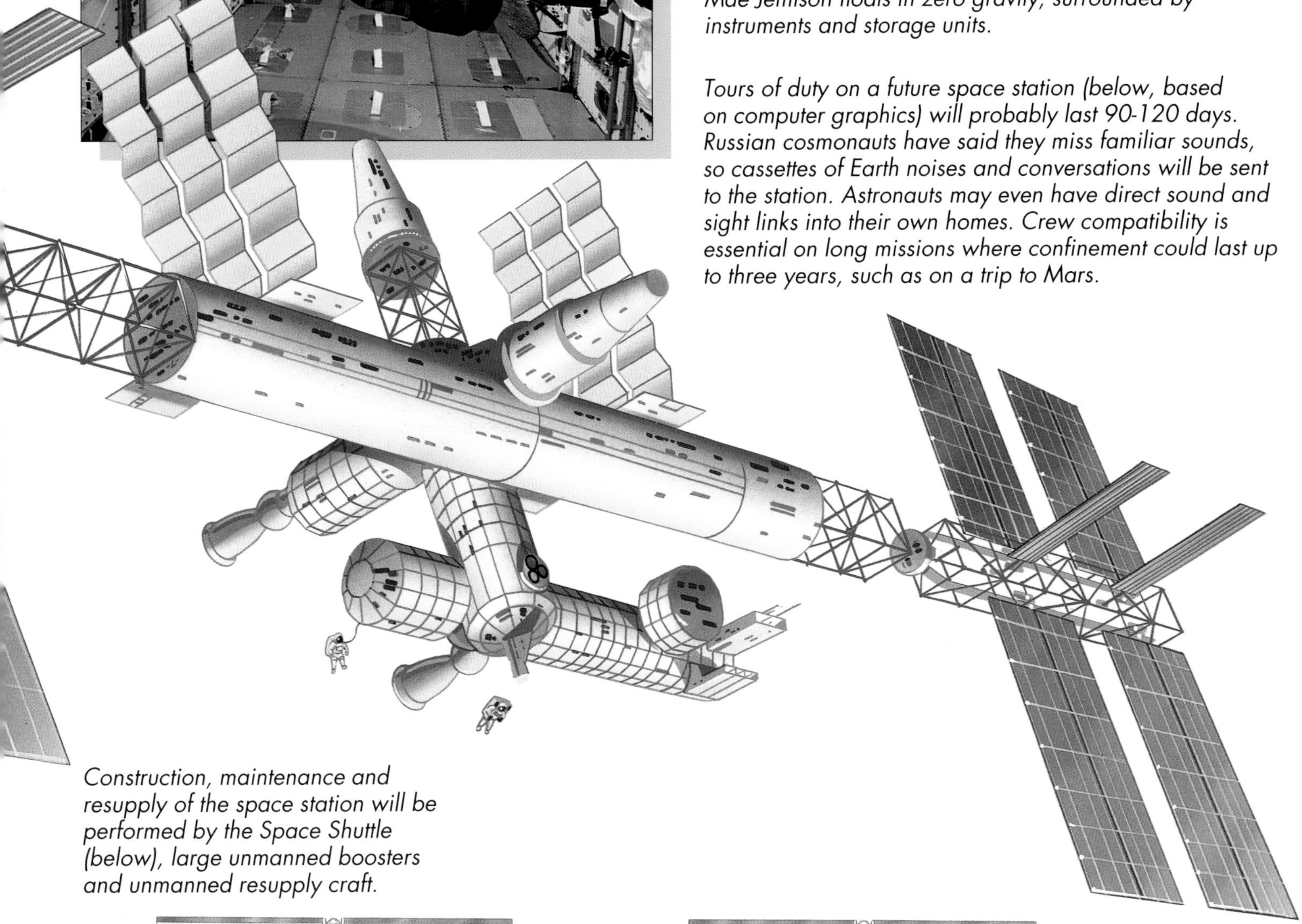

*Tours of duty on a future space station (below, based on computer graphics) will probably last 90-120 days. Russian cosmonauts have said they miss familiar sounds, so cassettes of Earth noises and conversations will be sent to the station. Astronauts may even have direct sound and sight links into their own homes. Crew compatibility is essential on long missions where confinement could last up to three years, such as on a trip to Mars.*

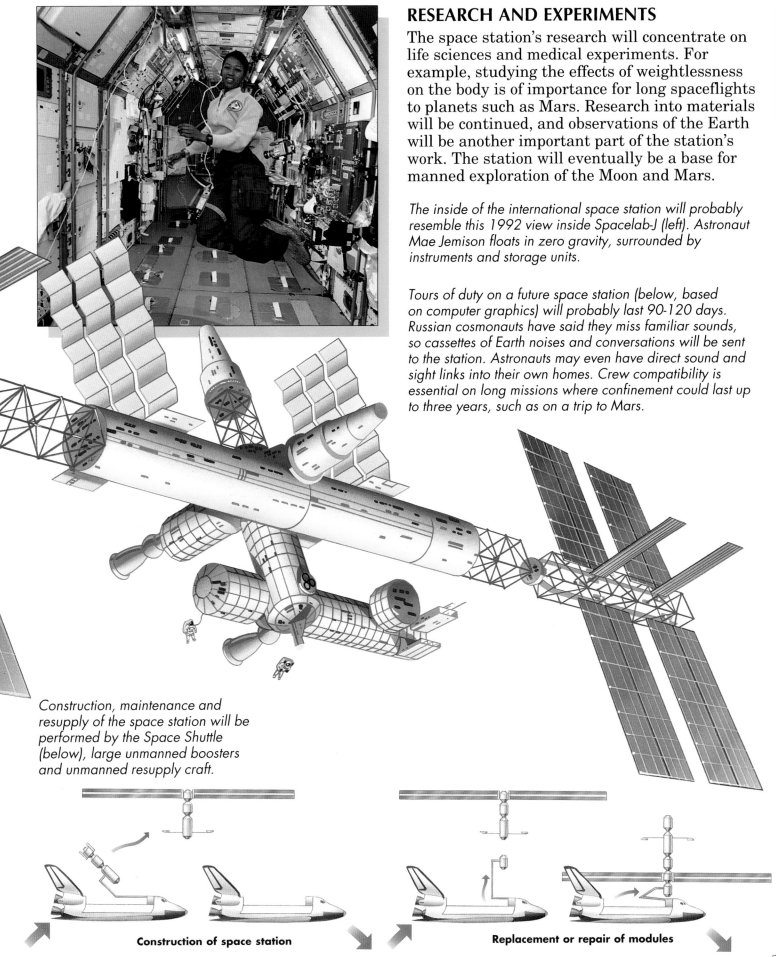

*Construction, maintenance and resupply of the space station will be performed by the Space Shuttle (below), large unmanned boosters and unmanned resupply craft.*

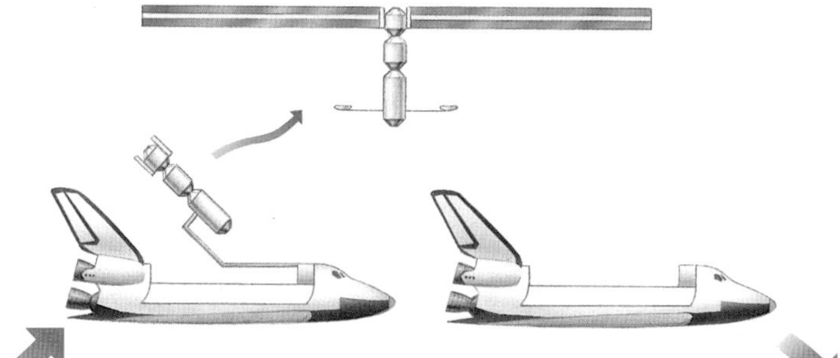

**Construction of space station**

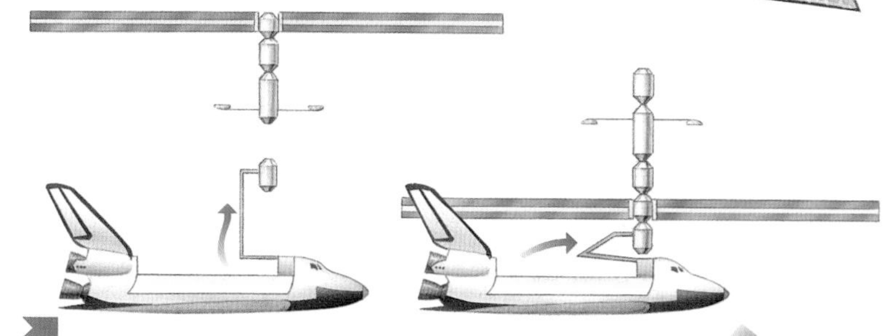

**Replacement or repair of modules**

# SPACE STATION *MIR*

**In February 1986 the Soviet Union launched the first section of a new space station. The station, called *Mir*, is made up of several modules that are taken into space and then joined together.**

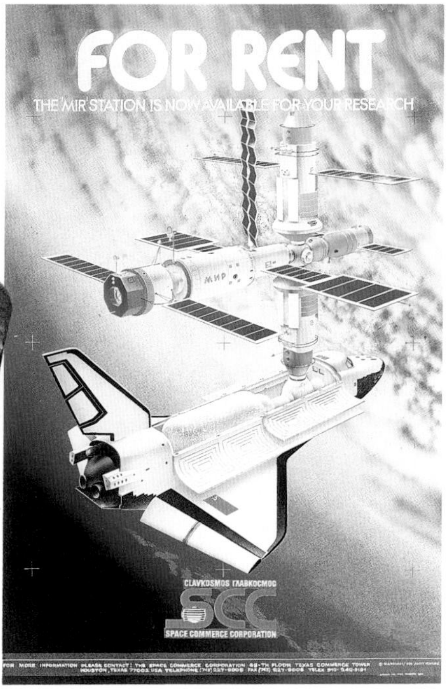
FOR RENT
THE MIR STATION IS NOW AVAILABLE FOR YOUR RESEARCH
SPACE COMMERCE CORPORATION

*For Rent. To help cover the costs of* Mir*, the Soviet space agency sold space for scientific experiments and flights for foreign cosmonauts.*

## A HOME IN SPACE

The main module contains only the crew quarters, flight controls and exercise equipment. Because they spend about six months in the zero gravity of space, the crew use the station's mini-gymnasium regularly so their muscles do not waste away. *Mir's* resident crew spend about six months in space before returning in a *Soyuz* spacecraft.

The first add-on section, called *Kvant-1*, was attached in 1987. It carried X-ray telescopes for studying a supernova, a rapidly-brightening star.

*When* Kvant-2 *was docked to* Mir*, it took with it a Manned Maneuvering Unit, or MMU, called* Ickarus*. This has enabled the cosmonauts to carry out repair and maintenance work in space.*

*There's very little room for the cosmonauts in* Mir*, or in the* Soyuz *spacecraft (above) that takes them to and from the station.* Mir *is not a tidy place, being full of equipment and the cosmonauts' personal items, such as music cassettes.*

## SCIENTIFIC EQUIPMENT

The main scientific equipment was to be added in four additional modules. The first of these, *Kvant-2*, was attached to *Mir* in December 1989. The last module docked to the station, called *Kristall*, is equipped with a large furnace for making metals in zero gravity.

The next modules, *Spectr* and *Priroda*, will study the Earth's natural resources and observe its atmosphere and outer space. They were designed to be carried into orbit by the Russian space shuttle *Buran*. It is more likely they will be sent up on unmanned launchers or the American Space Shuttle.

## THE FUTURE OF *MIR*

There were also plans to attach a medical lab to *Mir*. However, because of its cost, the future of *Mir* is increasingly dependent on international assistance, but plans for a *Mir 2* continue.

## A MAGNIFICENT ACHIEVEMENT

*Mir* is a magnificent achievement. The complex weighs 800 tonnes - before *Spectr* and *Priroda* are added - and has to generate its electricity from a huge array of solar panels. The top see-through scene shows *Mir* with *Kvant-2* and *Kristall* added, and a *Soyuz* spacecraft approaching. The lower picture shows a *Soyuz* and the other modules docked to the central docking unit.

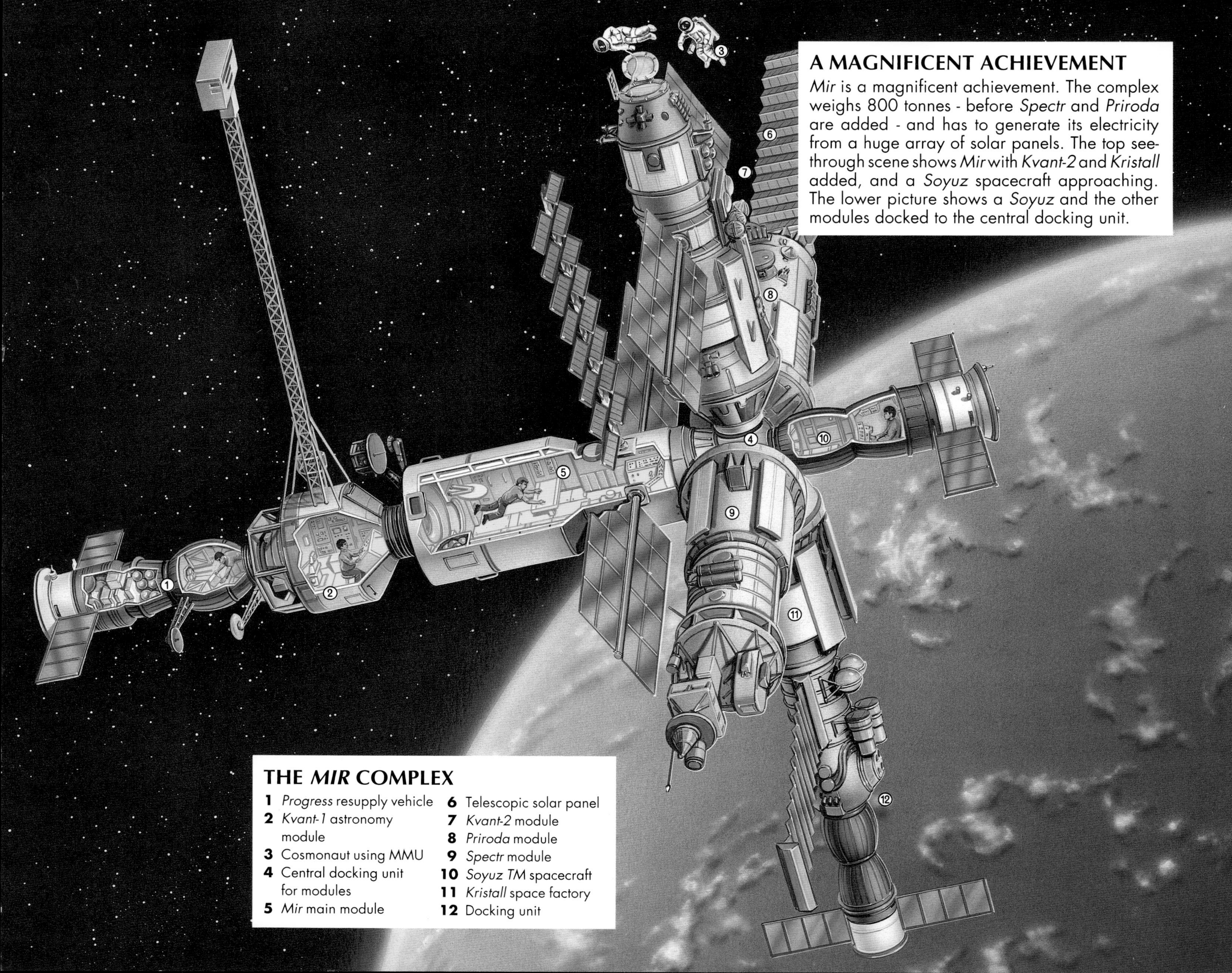

1
2
3
4
5
6
7
8
9
10
11
12


## THE *MIR* COMPLEX

**1** *Progress* resupply vehicle
**2** *Kvant-1* astronomy module
**3** Cosmonaut using MMU
**4** Central docking unit for modules
**5** *Mir* main module
**6** Telescopic solar panel
**7** *Kvant-2* module
**8** *Priroda* module
**9** *Spectr* module
**10** *Soyuz TM* spacecraft
**11** *Kristall* space factory
**12** Docking unit

# TO THE PLANETS

**In the early part of the next century, manned flight to Mars will be a real possibility. Mars is the closest planet to Earth which humans are capable of exploring. At the same time there are advanced plans to establish a research base on the Moon.**

## BASES ON THE SURFACE

Plans for the exploration of Mars have existed for many years: only the funds to pay for such an expensive trip have been lacking. When these are released then the first human explorers of Mars will be scientific researchers gathering as much information on their new environment as they can in the same way polar explorers did in the first South Pole bases.

Simulations of Mars bases are now being developed. Isolation experiments have existed in the Soviet Union since the 1960s, and in the USA *Biosphere 2* is a prototype of a future closed ecological system that might, one day, sit on the surface of Mars. Because of the huge distance to Mars (a two-year round trip compared to a week to the Moon and back), the explorers will stay on its surface for several weeks during each expedition.

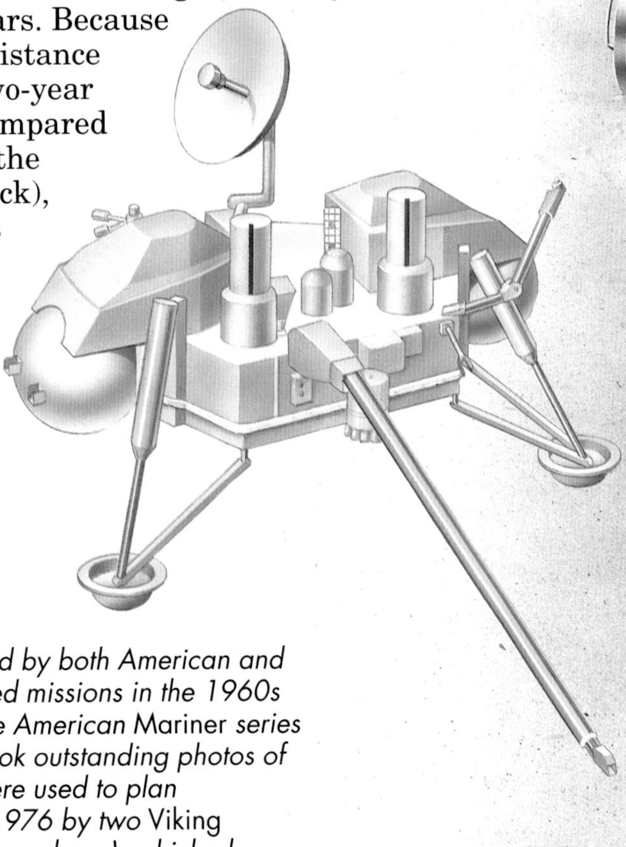

*Mars was visited by both American and Soviet unmanned missions in the 1960s and 1970s. The American Mariner series of spacecraft took outstanding photos of Mars. These were used to plan exploration in 1976 by two Viking spacecraft (shown above), which also carried orbiting vehicles.*

## MARS AND BEYOND

If people are born in the low gravity of the Moon or Mars, they might not be able to withstand the Earth's stronger gravity. Thus the first full-time Martians will be humans!

With Mars colonised and large bases on the Moon and in Earth orbit, the next target would probably be the asteroids for major mining operations, which will also be attempted on the Moon and Mars.

## MANNED EXPLORATION

Manned flights to the huge gas planets of Jupiter, Saturn, Uranus and Neptune will be possible in the latter part of the next century. They will not use today's power sources or nuclear fuel, but special engines and ion drives harnessing energy in a new way.

Manned landings on these planets will be impossible because of their terrific heat, gravity and storms. Nor do they have solid surfaces - they are big balls of gas held together by gravity. However, it might be possible to land on some of their moons for short periods.

*The first astronauts to return to the Moon will establish a research base (below). It will probably be manned by an international group of scientists. A permanent crew will remain on the surface for some months, carrying out scientific research. The base will also provide a test-station for later manned flights to Mars.*

# FUTURE DEVELOPMENTS

**The exploration of space has always been restrained by cost. As we move into the next century, it will still be a major factor. Predicting what will happen in space in the coming years is difficult, but as international co-operation increases, the future of manned spaceflight looks strong. So what might happen in the future?**

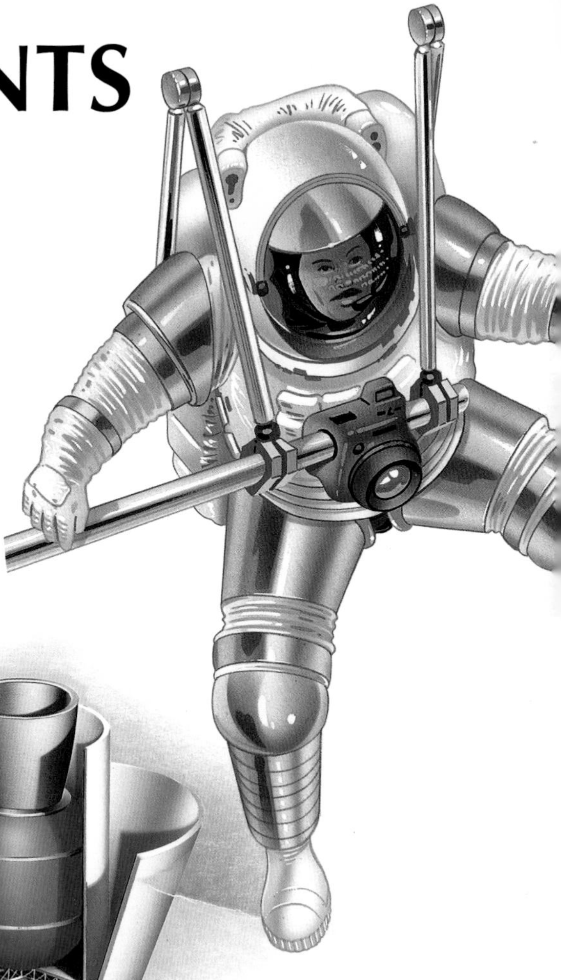

*A 21st century spacesuit (right). It has robot arms to assist the astronaut.*

## SPACECRAFT

Scientists are now designing the next generation of space launch systems. In particular they want to develop a 'Single Stage to Orbit' (SSTO) vehicle, such as the 'Delta Clipper'. This will leave the pad, climb straight into space and then be recovered intact and launched once more. This will be a fully reusable system, much cheaper but much heavier to place in orbit.

Other designs include unmanned air-launched vehicles similar to the X-15 rocket plane (see page 6), and 'space-planes' which use a normal runway, 'fly' into orbit and return to a runway landing. Engines like the *Star Trek* 'Warp Drive' are a long way into the future.

*The time-lapse photograph below shows the successful test of a small-scale prototype of a 'Single Stage to Orbit' vehicle, the DC-X 'Delta Clipper'.*

*In the future, 'penetrators' launched into comets, meteors and planetary surfaces (right) will obtain readings of their surface structure and temperature.*

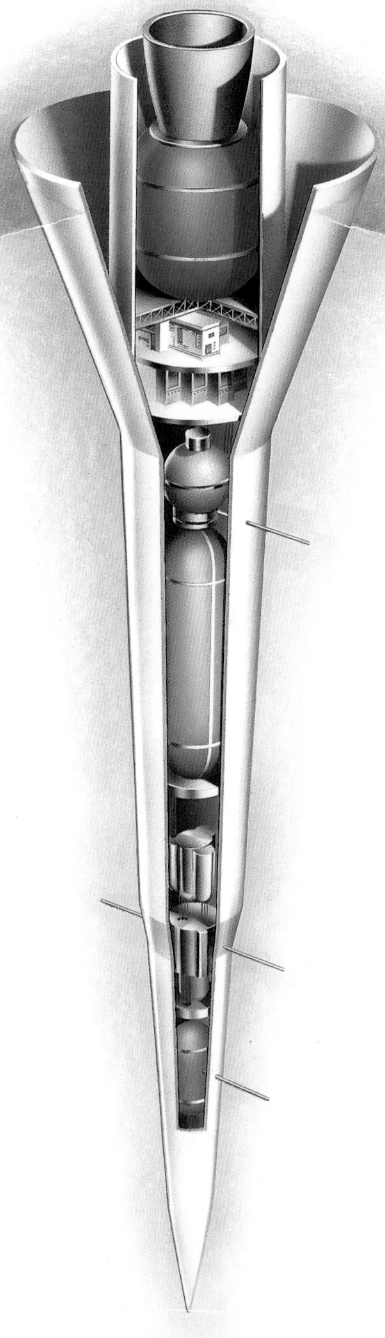

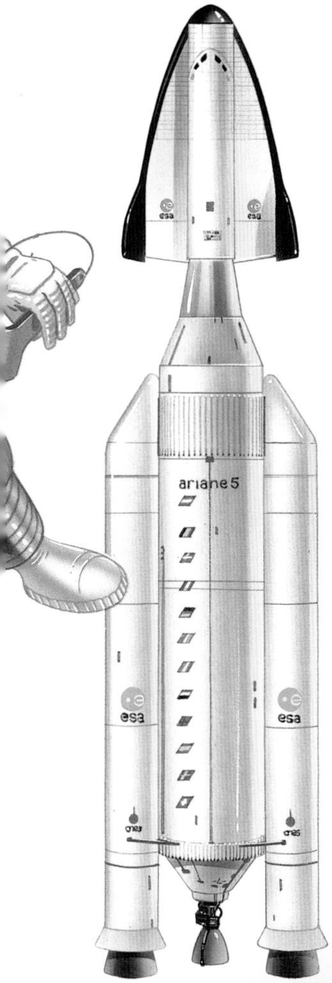
esa
ariane5
esa
esa

## BACK TO THE MOON

One of the next targets is a return to the Moon. Plans to resume the work begun by the pioneering *Apollo* landings are being developed, but actual steps on the lunar surface by the 13th human will not take place until the next century. However, one day there might be lunar cities, built on or below its surface.

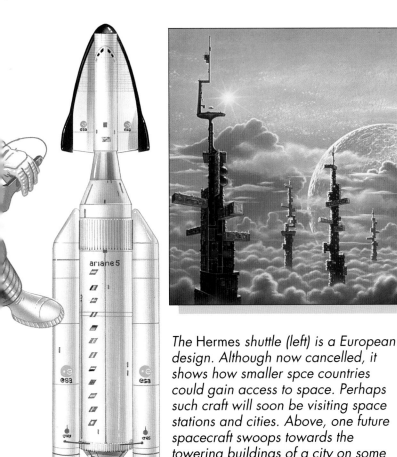

*The Hermes shuttle (left) is a European design. Although now cancelled, it shows how smaller spce countries could gain access to space. Perhaps such craft will soon be visiting space stations and cities. Above, one future spacecraft swoops towards the towering buildings of a city on some distant planet.*

## TOWARDS 2100

The Shuttle will remain the leading access for man into space for some time to come. Despite plans to develop a replacement vehicle to the Shuttle system, this is still many years in the future. But new designs and techniques are leaving the drawing board, and one day humans will boldly go where no-one has even thought to go before.

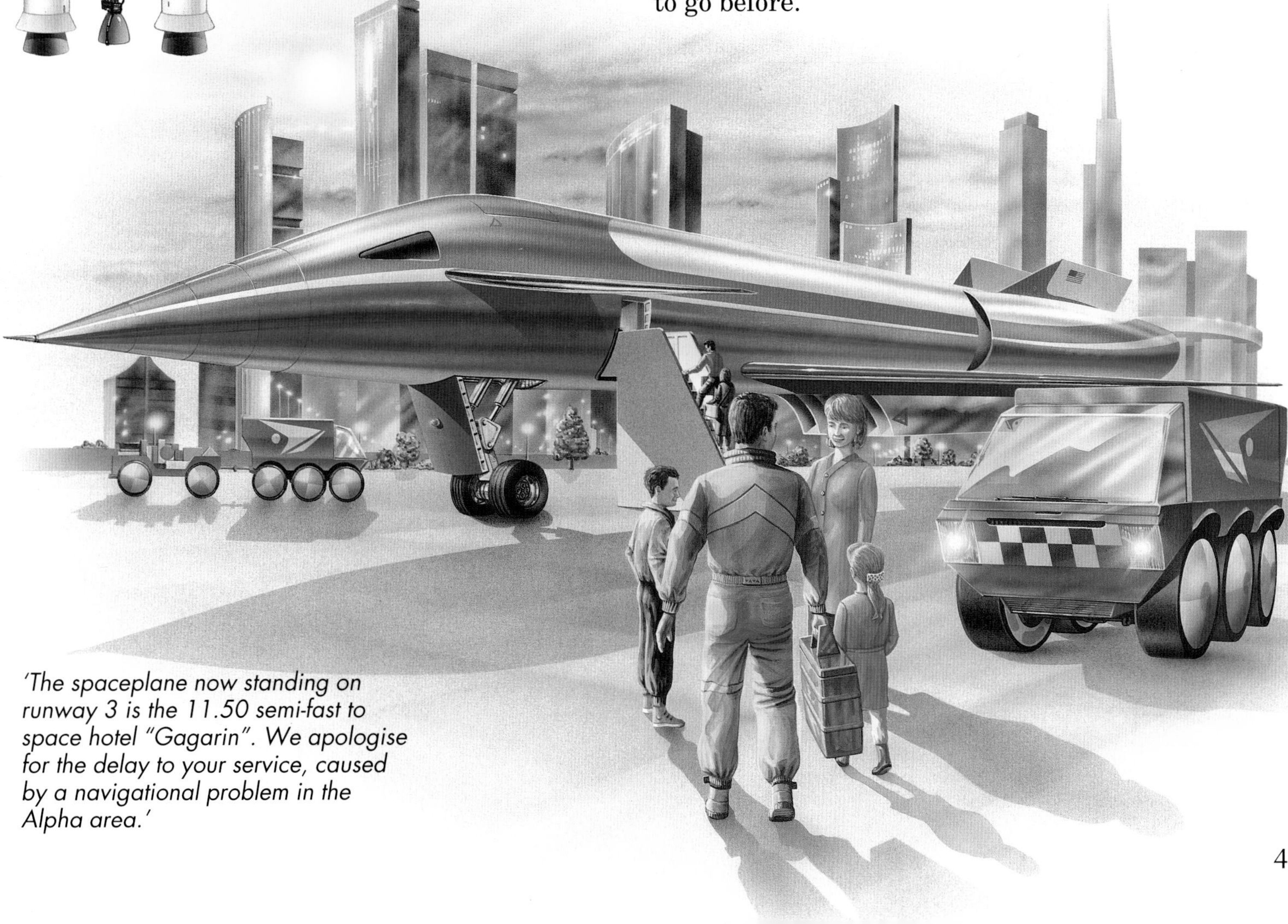

*'The spaceplane now standing on runway 3 is the 11.50 semi-fast to space hotel "Gagarin". We apologise for the delay to your service, caused by a navigational problem in the Alpha area.'*

# SPACE LOG

**There have been many historic events in the exploration of space. The following are just a few of the major milestones since the dawn of the 'space age' in 1957.**

### *1957*

**Oct** Soviet Union launches *Sputnik 1*, world's first artificial satellite

**Nov** *Sputnik 2* carries first living creature, *Laika* the dog, into space

### *1958*

**Jan** USA launches *Explorer 1*

**Feb** Launch of first weather satellite, USA's *Vanguard II*

**Oct** NASA - the National Aeronautics & Space Administration, controlling the USA's space programme - opens for business

### *1959*

**Apr** USA's first astronauts selected

**Sep** *Luna 2* crash-lands on Moon

### *1961*

**Apr** Yuri Gagarin first human in space

**May** Alan Shepard first American in space

**May** US President Kennedy sets Moon before 1970 as target for *Apollo* programme

### *1962*

**Jul** *Telstar 1*, first communications satellite

### *1963*

**Jun** Russian Valentina Tereshkova first woman in space

### *1965*

**Mar** Cosmonaut Alexei Leonov performs first spacewalk, in Earth orbit

**Jul** *Mariner 4* photographs Mars

### *1967*

**Jan** *Apollo 1* astronauts die in flash fire during simulated countdown

### *1968*

**Dec** *Apollo 8* orbits Moon

### *1969*

**Jul** Neil Armstrong and 'Buzz' Aldrin walk on Moon, during *Apollo 11* mission

### *1971*

**Jun** *Soyuz 11* cosmonauts lose lives during re-entry accident

**Jul** *Apollo 15* astronauts drive first car, the Lunar Rover, on Moon

### *1973*
**May** American *Skylab* space station launched

### *1975*
**Jul** American astronauts and Soviet cosmonauts meet and shake hands in orbit during joint ASTP mission

### *1976*
**Jul** *Viking 1* soft lands on Mars, followed in September by *Viking 2*

### *1977*
**Sep** Soviet space station *Salyut 6* launched, followed in 1982 by *Salyut 7*, paving way for *Mir* space station

### *1979*
**Mar** *Voyager 1* flies within 285,000 kilometres of cloud tops of Jupiter

**Dec** First European *Ariane* rocket launched

### *1981*
**Apr** *Columbia*, the first NASA Space Shuttle, launched into space

### *1983*
**Jul** *Pioneer 10* is first probe to pass Pluto, the outer planet of the solar system

### *1986*
**Jan** *Voyager 2* passes Uranus. Space Shuttle *Challenger* explodes 73 seconds after launch, killing crew of seven

**Feb** *Mir* space station launched

### *1988*
**Dec** Cosmonauts Titov and Manarov return to Earth after record flight of 366 days 18 hours 7 minutes - the first 'year' in orbit

### *1989*
**Oct** *Galileo* deployed for voyage to Jupiter

### *1991*
**May** Helen Sharman first Briton in space

### *1993*
**Dec** Hubble Space Telescope repaired

*Moments from the exploration of space (below). From left to right: Sketches by Konstantin Tsiolkovsky circa 1900. A US A-4 rocket (a captured German V-2) is launched in 1946.* Lunokhod 2 *and* Luna 21 *explore the Moon in 1973. The Space Shuttle Orbiter* Enterprise *separates from its Boeing 747 carrier aircraft for a test flight in 1977. A Mars Shuttle flies between planets, and the first landing by humans on Mars, in the 21st century.*

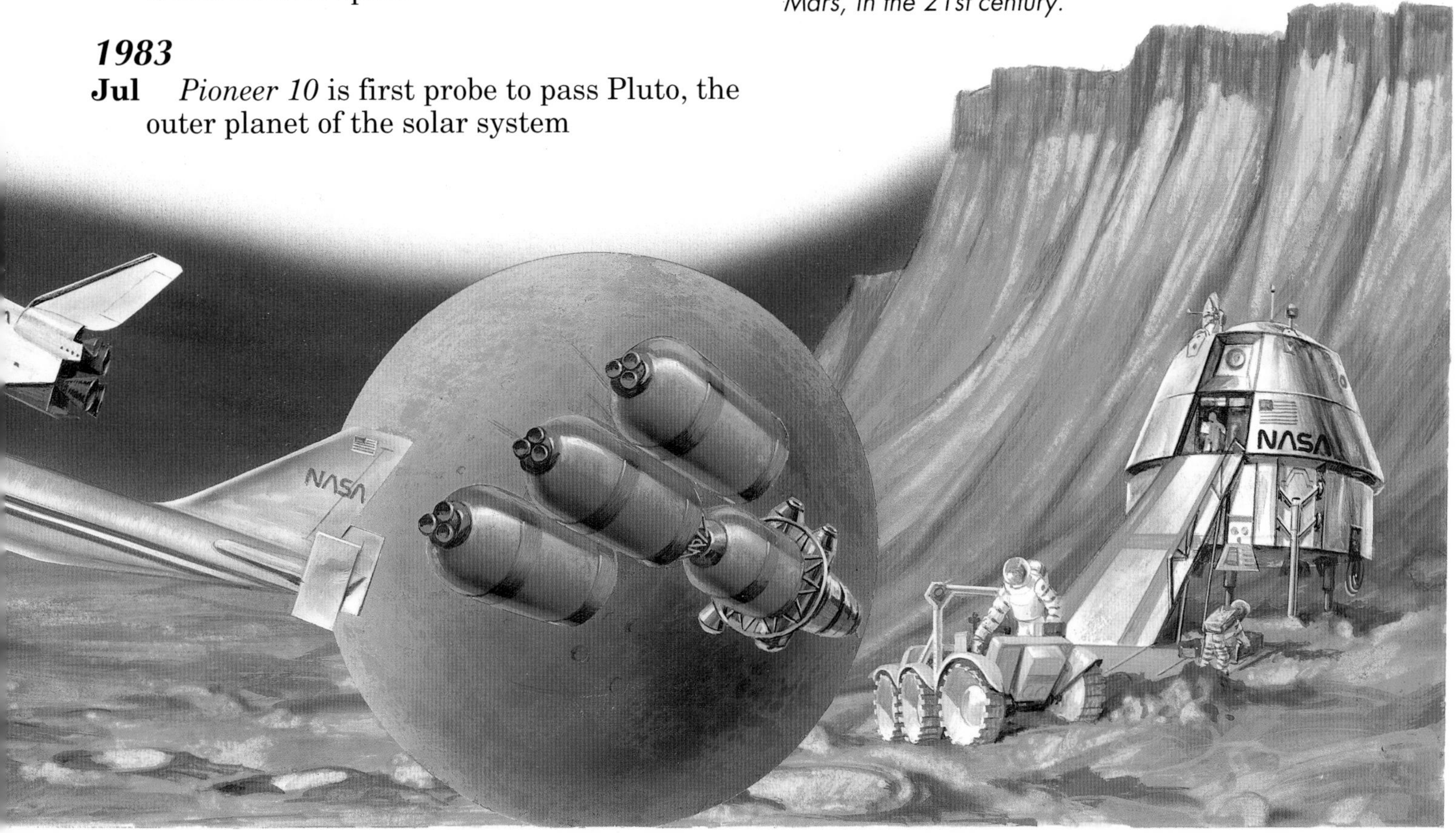
NASA
NASA

# INDEX

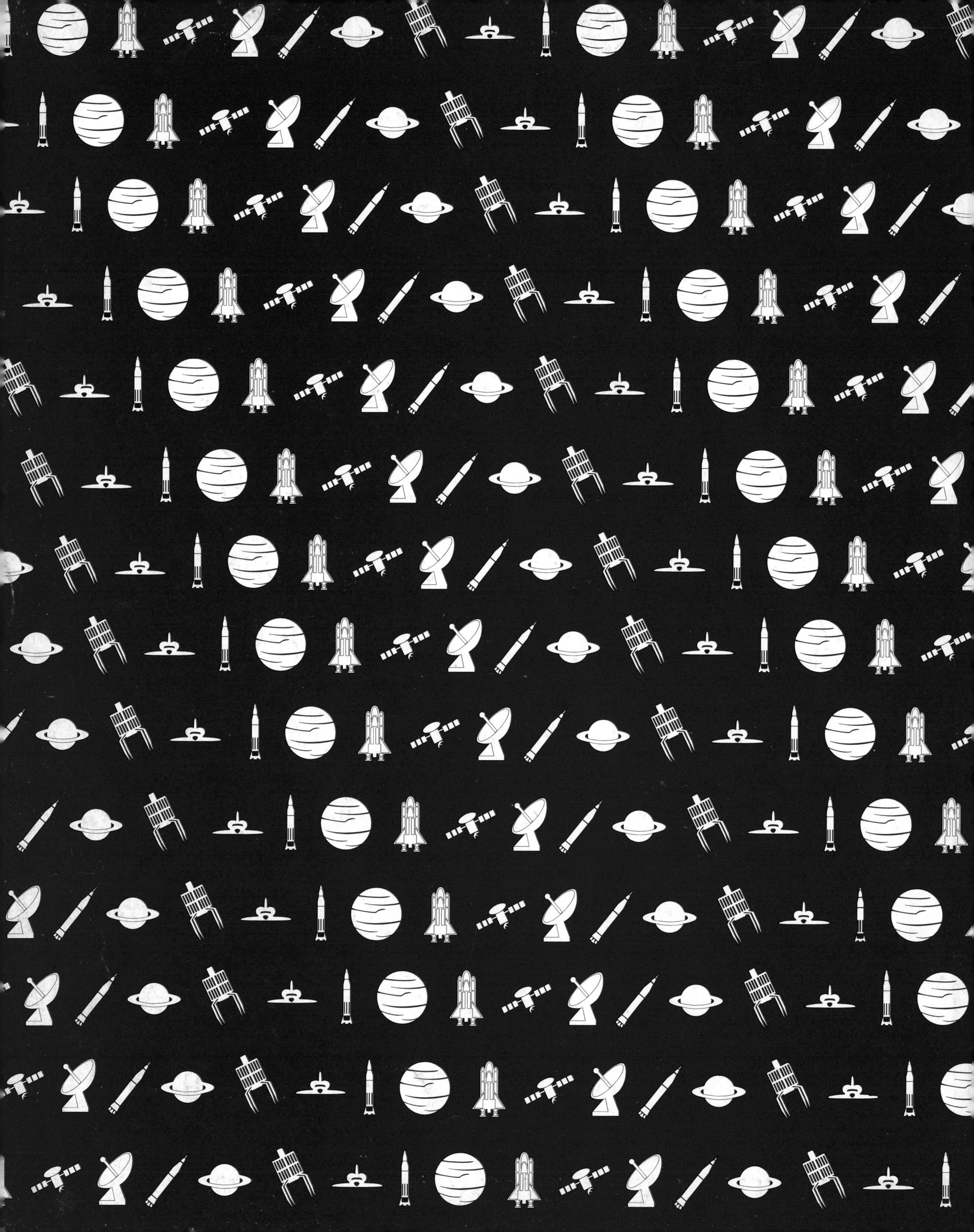